후다닥 하룻밤에 끝내는

NEW SMART

스크린영어 대표문장 2500

CHRIS SUH

MENTORS

후다닥 하룻밤에 끝내는
NEW SMART
스크린영어 대표문장 2500

2025년 7월 22일 인쇄
2025년 7월 29일 발행

지은이 Chris Suh
발행인 Chris Suh
발행처 MENTORS

경기도 성남시 분당구 황새울로 335번길 10 598
TEL 031-604-0025 FAX 031-696-5221
mentors.co.kr
blog.naver.com/mentorsbook
* Play 스토어 및 App 스토어에서 '멘토스북' 검색해 어플다운받기!

등록일자 2005년 7월 27일
등록번호 제2022-000130호
ISBN 979-11-94467-83-0
가 격 18,600원(MP3 무료다운로드)

잘못 인쇄된 책은 교환해 드립니다.
이 책에 게재된 내용의 일부 또는 전체를 무단으로 복제 및 발췌하는 것을 금합니다

머리말

실제 영어와 가장 유사한 스크린영어

스크린은 실제 살아있는 영어를 학습하는데 가장 좋고 쉽게 접할 수 있는 소스이다. 비록 대본이 있기는 하지만 교과서적인 교재영어를 벗어나 실제 영어를 만날 수 있는 좋은 기회이다. 물론 가장 좋은 방법은 미국 등 현지에 가서 지금 현재 그네들이 쓰는 무지막지한 실제영어에 부딪히며 체득해야 실제영어를 맛볼 수 있지만 현실적으로 다 그럴 수 없는 처지를 감안하면 스크린이야말로 가장 실제와 근접하다 할 수 있다.

<후다닥 하룻밤에 끝내는 스크린영어 대표문장 2500>

이런 점에 착안하여 이 책 <후다닥 하룻밤에 끝내는 스크린영어 대표문장 2500>은 가장 듣기 편한 로코 분만아니라 액션, 드라마, 그리고 귀에 쏙쏙 들어오는 디즈니 만화 등 거의 모든 장르의 영화에 자주 등장하는 2,500 여개의 문장들을 집중적으로 모아 보기 쉽게 알파벳 순으로 정리하였다.

한 두편을 집중적으로 파고 다양한 영화를 두루두루 봐야…

스크린영어를 공부할 때 주의할 점은 한 두개의 스크린만 골라서 집중적으로 파는 경우보다는 한 두편의 영화를 집중적으로 파고 나서 다른 영화들을 다수 접해서 많이 쓰이고 자주 나오는 빈출표현들을 자기 것으로 만들어야 된다는 점이다. 왜냐면 한 두편을 완전히 자기 것으로 만드는 것은 쉬운 일도 아니고 그래서 중도 포기하는 경우가 많기 때문이며, 또한 영화 전편에는 영어학습에 크게 도움이 되지 않는 표현들도 많이 들어 있어 효율성이란 측면에서도 문제가 생기기 때문이다. 따라서 한 두편을 독파하는 편식습관에서 벗어나 여러 편을 심도있게 공부하는게 지속성이나 효율성의 문제에서 더욱 합리적인 방법이 될 것이다.

빈출표현만 모아…

이 책에는 영화에 나오는 빈출표현들만 모았기 때문에 어떤 영화를 봐도 도움이 될 것이다. 스크린으로 영어를 정복하려는 많은 사람들에게 꼭 필요한 책이 되기를 바라며 글을 마친다.

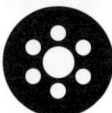

이 책의 특징

1. 로코, 액션, 드라마, 그리고 디즈니 만화에 자주 나오는 표현 2,500 표현을 알파벳 순으로 정리하였다.

2. 2,500개의 표현에는 우리말 번역뿐만 아니라 보충설명까지 있어 한번 읽은 표현은 잊혀지지 않도록 꾸며졌다.

3. 영화에 나왔던 명대사들을 부록에 정리하여 영화에 대한 기억을 되새길 수 있다.

이 책의 구성

❶ 총 2,500 여개의 문장들이 알파벳 순서로 사전식으로 정리되어 있다.

❷ 알파벳 구성은

A-H,
I-K,
L-S,
T-Y 등 총 4개의 파트로 대분되어 나뉘어져 있다.

❸ 각 파트가 끝날 때는 Check It Out!이 있어 실제 회화에서 스크린 대표문장들이 어떻게 쓰이는지 보여주고 있다.

이 책을 보는 법

알파벳 순으로 정리된 스크린영어 대표문장 2,500개가 보기 쉽게 정리되었다.

SCREEN TIPS란 제목으로 스크린에 자주 나오는 슬랭들을 모았다.

각 파트가 끝날 때마다 학습한 것을 확인해보기 위해 실제 회화에서 스크린영어 대표문장이 어떻게 사용되는지를 확인해본다.

마지막으로 기억에 남는 영화 속에 나오는 명대사를 수록하여 스크린영어뿐만 아니라 영화에 대한 기억을 다시 한번 느껴본다.

CONTENTS

A - H 001-432 — 007

- **A** 001-049
- **B** 050-065
- **C** 066-107
- **D** 108-223
- **E** 224-231
- **F** 232-246
- **G** 247-285
- **H** 286-432

Check it Out!

I - K 001-709 — 087

- **I** 001-680
- **J-K** 681-709

Check it Out!

L - S 001-274 — 211

- **L** 001-063
- **M-N** 064-124
- **O-R** 125-163
- **S** 164-274

Check it Out!

T - Y 001-680 — 263

- **T** 001-187
- **V-W** 188-414
- **Y** 415-680

Check it Out!

Supplement 영화속 명대사 — 383

후다닥 스크린영어
대표문장 2500

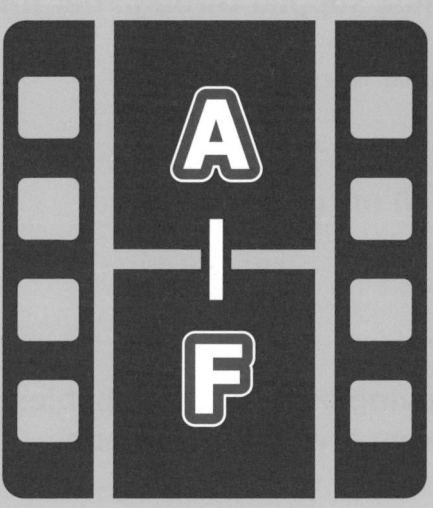

001

A fortune just slipped through her fingers.
그녀는 행운을 놓쳤어.

slip through one's fingers 기회를 놓치다, 잃어버리다

002

A toast to all my good friends.
내 모든 좋은 친구들을 위해 건배.

(A) Toast to sb[sth] …을 위해 건배

003

Actually, giving birth to three babies isn't that different from giving birth to one.
사실 아이 셋을 낳는 건 아이 하나를 낳는 거랑 다르게 없죠.

give birth 아이를 낳다

004

All in all, it was a pretty good childhood.
대체로 꽤 좋았던 어린시절이었어.

all in all 대체로

005
All of the students thought as much.
모든 학생들이 그럴거라 생각했어.

I thought as much 그럴거라 생각했어

006
All right, enough is enough. I'm not buying it.
좋아, 이젠 그만. 난 안 믿어.

Enough is enough 그만해, 더 이상은 안돼

007
All right, I'll do it myself.
좋아, 그럼 내가 하지.

All right(맞아, 그래 = Yes, Okay) Would that be all right? 그래도 괜찮을까?

008
All set.
준비 다 됐어요.

009
All this fibbing is gonna catch up with you.
이런 거짓말을 하면 들키기 마련이야.

catch up with 따라잡다, 이해하다, 만나다

010
All we can do is wait and hope for the best.
우리가 할 수 있는 건 기다리며 잘되기를 바라는게 전부야.

I hope for the best 잘 되기를 바래

011

Almost every guy I know has had sex with Jill. What a slut! 내가 아는 남자들 거의 다 질하고 자봤어. 헤픈 것 같으니라구!

012

Alright then, let's have it.
그럼 좋아, 어서 말해봐.

Let's have it 어서 말해봐 = Let me have it

013

Am I somebody you mess around with?
내가 네가 갖고 놀아도 되는 사람인거야?

mess around 빈둥거리다, 바람피다

014

And I knew I was fucked.
그리고 난 내가 엿먹었다는 것을 알게 됐어.

fuck sb하면 have sex라는 의미 외에, 「…을 엿먹이다」, 그래서 be fucked하면 「엿먹다」라는 뜻이 된다.

015

And if that's the case, why do I want this?
그게 사실이라면, 내가 왜 그걸 원하겠어?

(even) if that's the case 만약에 그렇다면

016

And if you mess up, if you fuck around, you're out. 그리고 네가 망쳐놓고 빈둥거리면 넌 끝이야.

fuck around 빈둥거리다, 개수작을 부리다

017
And on top of that, you're so normal.
게다가 넌 너무나도 평범해.
on top of that 게다가

018
And you're in denial!
그리고 넌 심리적으로 받아들이지 못하고 있는거야!
in denial 심리적으로 받아들이지 못하는 상태

019
Are these back in season again?
이것들이 다시 유행이야?
in season 유행인

020
Are we having fun yet?
일이 제대로 되는거야?
일이 잘 안되거나 계획대로 되지 않을 때 비아냥거리면서 하는 말

021
Are you (still) there?
듣고 있는거니?, 여보세요?

022
Are you and Chris friends with benefits?
너하고 크리스는 부담 없는 섹스파트너야?
friends with benefits 섹스파트너

023

Are you asking me out?
내게 데이트 신청하는거야?

ask sb out …에게 데이트 신청하다

024

Are you available?
시간돼?

025

Are you breaking up with me?
너 나와 헤어지자는거야?

break up은 남녀간에 사귀다가 헤어지는 것을 뜻하는 표현.

026

Are you coming on to me?
지금 날 유혹하는거야?

come on to sb 유혹하다, 꼬시다 come on 유혹

027

Are you decent?
들어가도 돼?(들어가도 될 만큼 입을 거 입고 있냐는 말)

028

Are you done with showering in the bathroom?
욕실에서 샤워 다했어?

Are you done (with)? (…을) 끝냈어?, 다했니?

029
Are you eating in or taking away today?
오늘은 안에서 드실래요 아니면 포장인가요?
take away 포장해가다

030
Are you going to be here tomorrow? I want to see you again. **너 내일 여기 올거야? 다시 보고 싶어서.**
be here[there] 오다, 가다 get there 도착하다, 성공하다

031
Are you gonna hook up with him?
걔 낚아서 잘거야?
hook up with sb …와 섹스하다

032
Are you kidding me? Where did I mess up?
정말? 내가 어디서 실수했는데?
Are you kidding (me)? 농담하는거야?, 웃기지마

033
Are you leaving so soon?
벌써 가려구?, 왜 이렇게 빨리 가?

034
Are you on crack?
너 약 먹었어?
be on crack 약을 하다

035
Are you out of your mind? What do you think you're doing? 너 제정신이야? 이게 무슨 짓이야?

What do you think you're doing? 이게 무슨 짓이야?

036
Are you ready to go?
갈 준비 다 됐어?

037
Are you ready to party?
신나게 즐길 준비됐어?

038
Are you saying he's a geek?
네 얘긴 걔가 괴짜라는거야?

039
Are you still there?
듣고 있는거니?, 여보세요?

040
Are you sure you'll be able to do it?
정말 너 그거 할 수 있어?

do it 그렇게 하다

041
Are you the person in charge here?
여기 책임자인가요?

be in charge of~ …을 책임지고 있다

042
Are you wearing makeup?
너 지금 화장하고 있는거야?

wear[do] makeup 화장하다

043
Aren't you supposed to get down on your knee or something?
무릎을 꿇거나 뭐 그래야 되는 것 아니예요?

get down on one's knees 무릎을 꿇다

044
As far as he knows, I play it straight.
그가 알고 있는 한 난 정석대로 했어.

play it straight 공정하게 행동하다

045
As far as I know, no one has been hurt.
내가 알기로는 아무도 다치지 않았어.

as far as I know 내가 알기로는

046
As I said, I was wrong. That's all. You can go.
내가 말했듯이, 내가 틀렸어. 그게 다야. 넌 가도 돼.

That's all 그게 다야 Is that all? 고작 그게 다야?

047

As it turned out, he had no choice.
나중에 밝혀진 것처럼 걘 선택할게 없었어.

as it turns[turned] out (나중에) 알고보니

048

As she walks down the aisle and the guests stand up.
걔가 통로로 걸어들어오자 하객들은 일어섰어.

walk down the aisle 복도를 걸어가다, 결혼하다

049

Ask Jim how to do it. He's done it before.
짐에게 하는 방법을 물어봐. 걘 전에 해봤거든.

He's done it 전에 해봤어, 또 저러네

SCREEN TIPS

말을 꺼내기 앞서, 혹은 중간에 저, 저기, 음 등 별 의미없는 말이다.

- **Look, ~** 이것 봐
- **Say, ~** 저기요, 있잖아
- **So, ~** 자, 그래서, 따라서
- **I mean, ~** 그러니까, 내 말은
- **See, ~ (또는 ~, see)** 이것봐, 자 보라구
- **Listen, ~** 들어봐
- **Well, ~** 저, 음
- **Hey, ~** 이봐
- **Now, ~** 자, 한데, 그런데
- **~, you know, ~** 있지, 음
- **~, like, ~** 그러니까, 음
- **What, ~** 뭐라고, 아니, 설마, 이런
- **Let's see, ~** 이것보라구
- **Let me think, ~** 생각 좀 해보자

050

Back off. You need time to cool down.

진정해. 넌 진정할 시간이 필요해.

Back off! 물러서!, 진정해!, 꺼져!

051

Be careful what you wish for.

뭘 원하는지 신중히 생각해.

052

Be ready to write down whatever she says.

걔가 뭐라든 다 적을 준비됐어.

write down 적어두다 (= get down, take down)

053

Beats me. Why don't you ask her?

몰라, 걔한테 물어봐.

Beats me 몰라, 내가 어찌 알아 = Search me

054

Been there done that.

(전에도 해본 것이어서) 뻔할 뻔자지.

055

Believe me, I only have eyes for one girl.
정말야, 난 한 여자만 사랑할 뿐이야.

Believe me 정말이야

056

Believe you me. You'll thank me for this one day. 내 말 믿어. 언젠가 내게 감사할거야.

Believe you me 정말 진심이야 *you는 강조하기 위해 쓴 것임.

057

Better left unsaid.
말 안하는 게 좋겠어, 입다물고 있는 게 도움이 될 때가 있어.

058

Big time.
그렇고 말고, 많이.

059

Bite me!
배째라!, 어쩌라구!, 꺼져!, 그만둬!, 네 맘대로 해!

060

Bottoms up! Let's get drunk!
위하여! 자 취하자!

Bottoms up! 원샷!, 위하여!

061
Break it down for me so I can understand.
설명해봐 내가 이해하도록 말야.

break it down for sb …에게 자세히 설명하다

062
But don't you take the easy way out.
곤란한 상황을 벗어나기 위해 쉬운 길을 택하지마라.

take the easy way out 곤경을 벗어나기 위해 쉬운 길을 택하다

063
But we're lucky to have him. Work it, Chris!
그가 있어 우린 행운이죠. 재능을 맘껏 발휘해봐, 크리스!

work it 영리하고 똑똑하게 일을 처리하다

064
By all means, read it when you have a free moment.
그럼, 시간있을 때 읽어봐.

by all means 그럼, 물론이지

065
By the way, what are you doing tonight?
근데, 오늘 밤에 뭐할거야?

What are you doing? 뭐해?, 시간 돼? What are you doing here? 여긴 웬일이야?

066
Call it even and move on with our lives.
비겼다 생각하고 각자 삶을 살자고.

move on with one's life (잊고) 새롭게 살아가다

067
Calm down. Don't try to bite my head off.
진정해. 나한테 화내려고 하지마.

bite one's head off 호되게 야단치다 take sb down 혼내주다

068
Calm down. We don't need to argue.
진정해. 다툴 필요 없잖아.

Calm[Stay] down 침착해, 진정해

069
Can I ask you something? How would you like my job?
뭐 좀 물어봐도 돼? 내 직업은 어떤 것 같아?

Can I ask you something[a question]? 뭐 좀 물어볼게

070
Can I get you something?
뭐 좀 사다줄까?, 뭐 좀 갖다줄까?

071
Can I have a quick word?
아빠, 잠깐 얘기할 수 있어요?
have a word (with sb) (…와) 얘기나누다 have words with 언쟁하다

072
Can I offer you a lift home?
집까지 차로 데려다줄까?
offer sb a ride[lift] 차 태워주겠다고 하다 want a ride[lift] 차 태워달라고 하다

073
Can you both live with that?
그 정도 선에서 둘이 합의하면 안돼?
can live with that 견딜만하다, 괜찮다

074
Can you cover for me? I just got an audition.
내 일 좀 봐줄래? 오디션이 있어서.
cover for sb …대신 일을 봐주다 = fill in for sb

075
Can you dial down your outburst please?
제발 네 감정을 좀 진정시킬래?
dial down 진정하다(calm down)

076

Can you excuse me for a minute? I got a quick phone call. 잠시 실례할게요. 빨리 전화할데가 있어서요.

Will you excuse me[us] for a moment? 잠깐 실례해도 될까요?

077

Can you give me a hand moving this bed?
이 침대 이동하는거 좀 도와줄래?

Can you give me a hand (~ing)? (…하는거) 나 좀 도와줄래?

078

Can you give me a hand?
좀 도와줄래?

079

Can you make it?
할 수 있겠어?, (제 시간에) 도착할 수 있겠어?

make it 1. 성공적으로 어떤 일을 해내다 2. …에 시간맞춰 참석하다 (make it to 장소/시간) 3. 생존하다

080

Can you shed some light on the current situation? 현재 상황을 해명해볼래요?

shed light on~ 밝히다, 해명하다

081

Can't beat that.
짱이야, 완벽해.

082
Can't believe you're going cold turkey for this chick.
이 여자를 위해 술을 끊다니 믿기지 않네.

go cold turkey 술이나 약을 끊다 cut off 술을 그만 마시다

083
Can't top that, Chris.
크리스, 난 최고야.

084
Can't we just put this behind us?
우리 이걸 잊을 수는 없을까?

put sth behind sb …을 잊다

085
Can't you do anything without my help?
넌 내 도움 없이는 아무 일도 못하니?

086
Cheers! You did a great job today.
위하여! 넌 오늘 일을 아주 잘했어.

Cheers (to you)! (너를) 위하여!

087
Chick won't stop dogging me, man.
여자들이 날 계속 괴롭히려고 해.

dog sb 괴롭히다

088

Chris, get out of here. You're fired.
크리스, 꺼지라고. 넌 해고야.

Get out of here! 나가!, 꺼져!, 웃기지마라! = Get out of my face!

089

Come and get it.
자 와서 먹자, 자 밥먹게 와라.

090

Come back and see us. Don't be a stranger.
다시 와서 얼굴 보자. 자주 보자고.

Don't be a stranger 자주 보자

091

Come on in and grab a drink.
어서 들어와 한잔 하자.

grab a drink 간단히 한잔하다

092

Come on you guys, is this really necessary?
이러지마, 얘들아. 꼭 이래야 돼?

093

Come on, keep going. You can't quit!
이봐, 계속하라고. 그만두면 안돼!

Keep going! 계속해!, 계속 가!

094
Come on, Ted. You always fall for that.
이봐, 테드. 넌 항상 그거에 넘어가잖아.

fall for sth 속아 넘어가다

095
Come over to my place[house].
우리 집에 들려.

096
Come to think of it, you should take a day off.
생각해보니까, 하루 휴가를 내는게 좋겠어.

come to think of it 생각해보니

097
Consider it done.
걱정마, 그렇게 할게, 문제없어.

098
Could I take a message?
메시지를 전해드릴까요?

leave the message with~ 메시지를 남기다 ⇔ take a message 메시지를 받다

099
Could you get it? I'm busy.
대신 문 좀 열어줄테야? 나 바빠.

get it 문을 열어주다, 전화를 받아주다

100
Could you give us a minute?
우리 좀 실례할게요.
Could you give me[us] for a moment? 잠깐 실례해도 될까요?

101
Could you hold?
잠시 기다리세요.

102
Could you lay off, please?
그만 좀 할래?

103
Could you please get out of my way?
제발 방해 좀 말아줄래?
get out of the[one's] way 방해가 되지 않다

104
Couldn't agree more.
정말 네 말이 맞아, 네 말에 전적으로 동의해.

105
Couldn't agree with you more.
정말 네 말이 맞아.

106

Cut me some slack.

좀 봐줘, 너무 몰아세우지마.

cut sb some slack …을 좀 봐주다

107

Cut the crap, you set this up, didn't you?

헛소리 그만해, 네가 꾸몄지, 그렇지 않니?

cut the crap 쓸데 없는 얘기 그만두다   shoot the crap 허튼 소리를 하다

 SCREEN TIPS

놀라거나 감탄할 때 쓰는 표현들 -1

- **(Oh my) Gosh!** 세상에!, 맙소사!
- **Oh, my God!** 세상에!, 하나님 맙소사!
- **(Oh,) My!** 이런!
- **(Oh) Boy** 1. 우와
  2. 이런 맙소사 [두려움, 나쁜 상황]
- **(Oh) Man!** 젠장!, 저런!
- **Shoot!** 이런!, 저런!, 아이쿠!
- **For crying out loud** 아이쿠, 이런
- **(Oh) My goodness** 어머나, 맙소사
- **Geez (혹은 Jeez)** 이런
- **Gee whiz** 세상에
- **My heavens!** 어머나!, 세상에!
- **Holy mother of God!** 에그머니나!
- **Dear me!** 어머나!, 아이고!, 저런!
- **Blimey!** 아이고 놀래라!
- **Whoops! / Oops!** 앗 이런!, 아이쿠!
- **Uh-oh** 어머 이를 어째 [앞 음절을 높게]
- **Wow!** 이야!, 우와!
- **Huh** 허, 흥 [의문, 놀람, 경멸, 무관심 등을 나타냄]

108

Deal with it. I have other problems to worry about. 알아서 처리해. 난 다른 문제들이 걱정야.

Deal with it 알아서 처리해라, 포기하고 받아들여라

109

Death doesn't put an end to love.

죽음도 사랑을 갈라놓지는 못해.

put an end to~ 끝내다(put a stop to~)

110

Deep down.

사실은 말야.

111

Did I miss it?

내가 놓쳤어?, 내가 못봤니?, 벌써 지나갔어?

112

Did my brother put you up to this?

내 형이 이걸 하자고 널 꼬득인거야?

put sb up to~ …에게 …하자고 하다

113

Did you and Chris ever get physical?
너하고 크리스하고 섹스해본 적 있어?

get physical 섹스하다, 폭력을 쓰다 get[do] a physical 건강검진을 받다

114

Did you fancy Chris the first time that you saw him?
크리스를 처음 볼 때 성적으로 끌렸어?

fancy sb 성적으로 끌리다

115

Did you get lost back there?
거기서 길을 잃었어?

get lost 길을 잃다(be lost)

116

Did you hear about the wedding? It's off.
결혼식 소식 들었어? 취소됐어.

It's off 관계가 끝났어, 취소되다

117

Did you hear that Ann got caught smoking by her father yesterday?
앤이 어제 담배 피우다 아버지한테 들켰다는 얘기 들었어?

get caught ~ing …하다 들키다

118

Did you know that he had recently split up with his wife? 걔가 최근에 이혼했다는 걸 알고 있었어?

split up with sb …와 헤어지다, 갈라서다

119

Did you land the job with the overseas client?
그 해외 고객 일을 따낸거야?

120

Did you see that chick that just came in?
야, 방금 들어온 그 여자 애 봤니?

121

Did you talk to Chris? How did it go?
크리스에게 말했어? 어떻게 됐어?

How did it go? 그건 어떻게 됐어?

122

Did you think you could betray me and just walk away? 날 배신하고 그냥 가버릴 수 있다고 생각했어?

walk away (from) …로부터 가버리다, 떠나다

123

Do I know you? You look familiar.
누구시죠? 인상이 낯익어서요.

Do I know you? 저 아세요?, 누구시죠?

124

Do I look like a guy who doesn't want to get married? 내가 결혼하고 싶어하지 않는 남자처럼 보여?

look like 마치 …처럼 보인다, …인 것 같다

125

Do it right.
제대로 해.

126

Do these people get paid for this?
이 사람들 이거 돈받고 하는거예요?

get paid 지불받다

127

Do what you like, love what you do.
네가 좋아하는 일을 하고 네가 하는 일을 사랑해라.

128

Do you have a problem with that?
그게 뭐 문제있어?, 그게 불만야?

129

Do you have enough to work on, this time of year? 연중 이맘 때에 할 일이 충분히 있나요?

this time of day 오늘 이맘때 this time of year 연중 이맘 때

130
Do you mean that?
진심이야?

131
Do you want me to go get them for you?
내가 가서 그것들을 가져올까?

Go get 'em 그들을 데려와, 그것들을 가져와라 = Go get them

132
Do you want me to look in on him?
내가 걔한테 잠시 들르기를 바래?

roll up 예고 없이 오다 = look in on sb

133
Do you want some company?
말동무가 필요해?

have company 일행이 있다, 손님이 있다

134
Do you want some more beer?
맥주 좀 더 먹을래?

Do you want some? 좀 먹을래? Do you want some more? 좀 더 먹을래?

135
Do you want to come over for dinner?
저녁 먹으러 올래?

온 목적을 말하려면 come over for~라고 하면 된다.
참고로 Sth come over sb하게 되면 …가 엄습하다라는 의미

136
Do you want to say yes now, or drag it out so you look cool? 지금 예스할래 아님 쿨하게 보이려고 시간을 끌거야?

drag out 시간을 끌다 = stall

137
Do your best and let the chips fall where they may. 최선을 다하고 결과에 상관없이 소신대로 행동해.

let the chips fall where they may 결과에 상관없이 소신대로 행동하다

138
Does it[that] work for you?
네 생각은 어때?, 너도 좋아?, 너한테 괜찮아?

Sth works for~ …가 …에게도 괜찮냐(Sb works for~ …을 위해 일하다)

139
Does that ring a bell?
뭐 기억나는거 있어?

ring a bell 기억이 나다

140
Does this afternoon work for you?
오늘 오후 괜찮아?

Does it[that] work for you? 네 생각은 어때?, 너도 좋아?

141
Doing okay?
잘지내?, 괜찮아?

142
Don't act that way. I believe you heard me.
그런 식으로 행동하지마. 내가 말했잖아.

I believe you heard me 내가 말했잖아 I don't think you heard me 내 말 못들었구만

143
Don't ask me why, but I got a feeling there's a connection.
이유는 묻지마, 그런데 뭔가 관련이 있는 것 같아.

Don't ask me why 이유는 묻지마

144
Don't be ridiculous. He isn't gay.
말도 안돼. 걔는 게이가 아냐.

Don't be ridiculous 말도 안돼, 웃기지마 This is ridiculous 이건 말도 안돼

145
Don't be silly. Why would I do that?
웃기지마. 내가 왜 그러겠어?

Don't be silly 바보같이 굴지마

146
Don't be so hard on yourself. It wasn't your fault.
너무 자책하지마. 네 잘못이 아냐.

be hard on oneself …을 힘들게 대하다 = give oneself a hard time

147
Don't be so sure.
모르는 소리.

148
Don't be such an arse.
멍청이처럼 굴지마.

149
Don't be surprised if I just pop in unannounced just to check up. 불시에 잠깐 확인하러 와도 놀래지마.

pop in(to) 잠시 들어가다 pop down 잠시 다녀가다 pop to~ 잠시 …에 가다

150
Don't bitch about it.
그거 가지고 징징대지마.

bitch about~ 불평하다

151
Don't blow it out of proportion.
지나치게 부풀리지마, 너무 과장하지마.

blow sth out of proportion 과장하다

152
Don't blow me off.
나 무시하지마.

blow sb off …을 무시하다, 골탕먹이다

153
Don't bother. I'm not hungry.
신경쓰지마. 나 안 배고파.

Don't bother 그러지마, 괜한 고생마 Don't bother me 귀찮게 하지 말고 저리 가

154
Don't bullshit me, Chris.
나한테 구라치지마, 크리스.
bullshit 허튼 소리를 하다 go blah 허튼 소리를 하다

155
Don't call me names!
험담하지마!, 욕하지마!
call sb names …을 험담하다, 욕하다

156
Don't do anything I wouldn't do on our blind date. **소개팅에서 바보 같은 짓 하지마.**
Don't do anything I wouldn't do at[on]~ …에서 바보 같은 짓 하지마

157
Don't even think about (doing) it.
꿈도 꾸지마, 절대 안되니까 헛된 생각하지마.

158
Don't even think about it. We've got a lot of work to do. **절대 안돼. 할 일이 너무 많아.**
Don't even think about it 꿈도 꾸지마

159
Don't feel so bad about it.
너무 속상해하지마, 너무 맘아파 하지마.

160
Don't flatter yourself. I'm just ignoring you.
착각마. 난 널 무시하고 있는거야.

flatter oneself 착각하다, 잘난 척하다

161
Don't freak out, OK?
놀라지마, 알았어?

freak out 놀라다, 놀래키다

162
Don't get all snooty with me just because you're so busted. 넌 딱 걸렸으니 내게 거만하게 굴지마.

snooty 오만한   be busted 체포되다, 걸리다

163
Don't get hung up on it.
너무 신경쓰지마.

get[be] hung up on[about]~ 잊지못하다, 매우 걱정하다, 신경쓰다

164
Don't get me started.
난 빠질래, 그 얘긴 꺼내지도 마.

165
Don't get me wrong, but Clay doesn't seem smart. 오해하지마, 하지만 클레이는 똑똑해 보이지 않아.

Don't get me wrong, but~ 오해하지마, 하지만…

166
Don't get your hopes up yet.
아직 너무 기대하지마.

get one's hopes up 기대하다

167
Don't give it a second thought.
걱정하지마, 두번 생각할 필요없어.

give it a second thought 걱정하다, 자꾸 생각하다

168
Don't give me that look. It's written all over your face.
그런 표정 짓지마. 네 얼굴에 다 쓰여있다고.

Don't give me that look 날 그런 식으로 쳐다보지마 = Don't look at me like that

169
Don't give me that. It's total bullshit.
그런 말 마. 완전히 거짓말이잖아.

Don't give me that! 그런 말 마!

170
Don't go behind my back.
뒤통수치지마.

go behind one's back …의 뒤통수를 치다

171
Don't go there.
그 문제는 언급하지마, 그 얘긴 하지마.

172
Don't hang up on me like that.
그런 식으로 전화 끊지마.

hang up on sb 도중에 전화를 끊다

173
Don't hold your breath.
기대하지마, 기다리지마.

hold one's breath 숨을 멈추다, (두려움, 기대 속에) 숨을 죽이다

174
Don't leave. Let me make it up to you.
가지마. 보상해줄게.

make it up to sb …에게 보상하다

175
Don't let it bother you.
너무 신경 쓰지마, 그냥 무시해.

bother 신경쓰이게 하다, 괴롭히다

176
Don't let me down.
(믿었던 상대방이 실망시켰을 때) 날 실망시키지마.

let sb down …을 실망시키다

177
Don't lie to me. I've seen you flirt with him.
거짓말 마. 네가 그 남자랑 집적대는 걸 봤어.

flirt with sb …에 집적대다

178
Don't lie to me. You committed a murder.
거짓말 마. 넌 살인을 저질렀어.
commit a crime[murder] 범죄[살인]를 저지르다

179
Don't look at me. It was his idea.
나 아니야. 걔 생각이었어.
Don't look at me 내가 안그랬어

180
Don't make it any harder than it already is.
더 이상 일을 힘들게 하지마라.
make it harder than it already is 지금보다 일을 더 힘들게 하다

181
Don't make me feel bad for doing my job.
내 일을 한 것뿐인데 날 기분나쁘게 하지마.
do one's job …의 일을 하다

182
Don't make this hard for me.
이걸 더 힘들게 만들지 말아줘.
make ~ hard …을 어렵게 하다

183
Don't mention it. I'm just doing my job.
무슨 말씀을. 그냥 내 일을 할 뿐인데.
Don't mention it 천만에요, 뭘요 = Not at all

184
Don't mess with me.
나 건드리지마.

mess with 쓸데없이 간섭하다, 속이거나 말썽을 일으키다

185
Don't pass up your chance.
기회를 놓치지 마라.

pass up one's chance …의 기회를 놓치다

186
Don't play dumb[coy] with me.
날 바보 취급하지마, 내가 바보같아.

play dumb 멍청한 척하다

187
Don't play games with me.
날 갖고 놀 생각 마, 나한테 수작부리지마.

play games with~ …에게 수작부리다

188
Don't play hard to get with him.
걔한테 빼지마.

play hard to get with sb …에게 튕기다, 비싸게 굴다

189
Don't pull my leg about serious things.
중요한 문제로 날 놀리지마.

pull one's leg …을 놀리다 pick on sb 괴롭히다

190

Don't pull that with me. I won't tolerate it.
내게 그걸 강요하지마. 난 참지 않을거야.

Don't pull that with me! 강요하지마!

191

Don't push your luck!
너무 행운을 믿지마!, 너무 설치지마!

push[press] one's luck 운을 과신하다, 너무 설쳐대다

192

Don't put yourself down.
자신을 낮추지마.

193

Don't say a word. Pretend it never happened.
한 마디도 하지마. 없었던 걸로 해.

pretend it never happened 전혀 그런 적 없던 걸로 하다

194

Don't screw with me.
나한테 장난치지마.

195

Don't spy on me.
날 훔쳐보지마.

spy on 몰래 보다, 감시하다

196
Don't sweat it!
(별일 아니니) 걱정하지 마라!, 그런 일로 진땀빼지마!, 신경쓰지마!

197
Don't take it out on me.
내게 분풀이 하지마, 왜 나한테 화풀이야.

take it out on sb …에게 화(분)풀이하다, 몰아붙이다

198
Don't take it personally.
기분 나쁘게 받아들이진마.

199
Don't take it personally. He's scared to climb down.
기분나쁘게 듣지마. 걘 등산하는 걸 무서워해.

200
Don't take no for an answer.
상대방이 거절해도 끈질기게 설득해라.

201
Don't take this the wrong way, but how old are you?
이상하게 받아들이지 말아, 몇 살이야?

Don't take this the wrong way 오해하지마 = Don't take this wrong

202
Don't tell anyone about this. Promise?
이거 누구한테도 말하지마. 정말이야?

(You) Promise? 정말이야?

203
Don't tell her about it. It's like asking for trouble.
그 여자에겐 입도 뻥긋하지마. 괜히 긁어 부스럼 만드는 거라구.

ask for trouble 사서 고생하다

204
Don't tell me what to do!
나에게 이래라 저래라 하지마!

205
Don't tell me.
설마, 그런 말마, 말하지마.

206
Don't touch the phone! I'll get it.
전화받지마! 내가 받을거야.

get it의 형태로 전화가 올 때 옆의 사람에게 「전화를 받아달라고」(Will you answer the phone?) 할 때 쓴다.

207
Don't try to cheer me up.
나를 기운나게 하려고 하지마.

cheer sb up …을 기운나게 하다

208
Don't try to pin it on me!
나한테 뒤집어 씌우지마!

pin~on sb …을 …에게 뒤집어 씌우다

209
Don't turn your back on him.
걔한테 등을 돌리지마.

turn your back on sb 배신하다

210
Don't waste your time.
시간낭비하지마, 시간낭비야.

211
Don't worry about it. It's not a big deal.
걱정하지마. 별거 아니야.

Don't worry about sb[sth] …은 걱정마

212
Don't worry! It's no big deal.
걱정마! 별거 아냐.

No big deal 별거 아냐 What's the big deal? 무슨 큰일이라도 있는거야?, 무슨 상관야?

213
Don't worry, you can count on me.
걱정마. 나만 믿어.

Don't worry 걱정마(Don't worry about a thing)

214
Don't worry. I'll do them.
걱정마, 애들은 내가 볼게.
do the kids 아이들을 돌보다

215
Don't worry. I'll get it done for you.
걱정마. 널 위해 해낼테니까 말야.
Don't worry 걱정마

216
Don't worry. You're doing the right thing.
걱정마. 넌 일을 제대로 하고 있어.
You're doing the right thing 일을 제대로 하고 있어

217
Don't you dare bail on me!
네가 어떻게 나를 바람맞힐 수 있니!
Don't you dare! 그러기만 해봐라! Don't you dare+V 멋대로 …하지마라

218
Don't you dare!
당치도 않아!, 까불지마!

219
Don't you think he went a little overboard?
걔가 좀 심했다고 생각하지 않아?
overdo 지나치게 하다 go overboard 너무하다

220

Drive carefully. Watch out for ice.

운전 살살해. 얼음 조심하고.

Watch out! 조심해 watch out for sb[sth] 조심하다

221

Dude, back off. I called dibs on Stephanie.

이봐, 물러서. 스테파니는 내가 찍었어.

have got dibs on …을 찜하다

222

Dude, what are you doing?

야, 너 지금 뭐해?

223

Duly noted. I will check up on it.

알았어. 확인해볼게.

Duly noted (무슨 말인지) 알아

SCREEN TIPS

놀라거나 감탄할 때 쓰는 표현들 -2

- **Look at you!** 얘 좀 봐!(감탄/비난)
- **Look at that!** 저것 좀 봐!(감탄/비난)
- **Mazel tov!** (유대인) 축하해!
- **Great Scott!** 이럴 수가!, 원 세상에!(감탄/놀람)
- **For God's[Christ's] sake**
  제발!, 지독하네!, 너무하는구만!
- **Thank God[goodness]** 다행이야
  = Thank the Lord
- **My(Good) Lord!** 맙소사!, 아이구!
- **God forbid!** 그런 일이 일어나지 말기를!
  (Heaven forbid!)
- **God bless you!** 감사하기도 하지!
  [누군가 재채기를 했을 때에도]
- **blah blah blah** 어쩌구저쩌구, 기타 등등
- **Whoa!** 상대방에게 진정하라는 의미로 하는 말

224

Easier said than done.
말이야 쉽지.

225

Either do your job or go home. Leave me out of it. 일을 하던지 집에 가. 난 빼주고.

Do your job 네 일이나 잘해, Do your job right 차질없이 일 제대로 해라

226

Everything will work out all right.
모든 일이 다 잘 해결될거야.

(Things, It) work out 곤란한 상황이 나아지다, 해결되다

227

Everything will work out for the best.
결국에는 다 잘될거야.

work out for the best 결국 잘 되다 turn out for the best 일이 잘 풀리다

228
Excuse me, I have a question for you.
실례지만 질문할 게 있는데요.

Excuse me, 실례지만, 저기.

229
Excuse me. Can I help you with something?
실례지만 뭐 좀 도와드릴까요?

Can I help you (to)? (그거 하는거) 도와줄까?

230
Excuse me? Could you repeat that?
뭐라고요? 다시 한번 말해줘요.

Excuse me?하면 상대방에게 "다시 말해달라"는 의미로 I'm sorry?, Come again?, Pardon? 등과 같은 뜻이다.

231
Excuse us, we need to go.
실례해요, 우리 가야 돼서요.

Excuse us 우리 지나갈게요, 잠깐 자리를 비켜주세요, (자리를 떠나며) 실례지만

SCREEN TIPS

짜증날 때 내뱉은 욕설들.

- **Holy shit [crap]!** 젠장!, 빌어먹을!
- **(Oh,) Crap** 이런!
- **(God) Damn it!** 젠장헐!
- **Darn (it)!** 에잇!, 이런!
- **Bloody hell!** 젠장헐!
- **Up yours!** 젠장헐!
- **Fuck it!** 제기랄!, 젠장!, 닥쳐!
- **Blow me!** 젠장헐!
- **Sod off!** 꺼져!
- **Sod it![that!]** 제기랄!, 빌어먹을!
- **Sod 'em all!** 빌어먹을!, 제기랄!
- **Bugger off!** 꺼져!
- **Bugger (it)!** 제기랄!
- **Oh, bollocks!** 엿같은 소리하네!, 헛소리마!

232

Fair enough. I'll leave you in peace.
좋아. 널 편안하게 놔둘게.

Fair enough 좋아, 됐어, 이제 됐어, 알았어

233

Far be it from me to call her a liar.
걔를 거짓말쟁이라고 부를 맘은 조금도 없지만.

far be it from me to+V 난 …할 생각이 추호도 없어

234

Fill in the blanks.
빈칸을 채우시오, 네가 맞춰봐, 결론이 어떻게 되는지 감이 잡혀.

235

Fine. Fine. But you do all the talking.
좋아. 좋아. 하지만 네가 다 설명해야 돼.

do (all) the talking 설명하다, 얘기하다

236
Fire away! I can handle it.
어서 물어봐! 내가 처리할 수 있어.

fire away 질문하다

237
First things first. What the hell is that?
중요한 것부터 하자. 이게 도대체 뭐야?

What is it[that/this]?의 강조형으로 What과 is 사이에 the hell을 삽입한 경우

238
First time since the breakup.
헤어진 후로 처음이야.

breakup 헤어짐, 이별

239
For all I know, that guy's my soul-mate.
아마도 저 남자가 내 소울메이트일지 몰라.

for all I know 아마도 …일지도 몰라 for all intents and purposes 사실상

240
For crying out loud, I was at my girlfriend's place. 세상에, 난 여친 집에 있었다구.

For crying out loud 세상에나

241
For what it's worth, I plan to prove him wrong.
모르긴해도, 난 걔가 틀렸다는 것을 증명할 계획이야.

prove sb wrong …가 틀렸음을 증명하다

242
For what? Leaving or coming back?
뭐 때문에? 떠날거야 돌아올거야?

For what? 뭐 때문에?

243
Freeze! Stop right there or I'll shoot!
꼼짝마! 거기 그대로 있어 그렇지 않으면 쏜다!

stop right there 꼼짝마, 그만해

244
From here on in, everything will be a whole lot easier. 이제부터는, 모든게 다 훨씬 쉬워질거야.

from here on in[out] 이제부터는

245
Fuck me! I didn't do my homework.
빌어먹을! 숙제를 안했네.

Fuck me!는 "빌어먹을!," "젠장!," "꺼저!," 그리고 Fuck'em은 "빌어먹을," "난 신경안써" 등의 의미로 쓰인다.

246
Fuck you! Weren't you my friend?
꺼지라고! 너 내 친구 아니었냐?

Fuck you!하게 되면 "염병할!," "제기랄!"이라는 의미로 Blow me!나 Up yours!와 같은 뜻이다.

247
Gee, how could that be?
이런, 어떻게 그럴 수 있어?

248
Geez, we're gonna be late, sweetie.
이런, 우리 늦겠어, 자기야.

249
Get a grip on yourself. You're acting crazy.
진정해. 너 행동이 이상해.

Get a grip! 정신차려!, 진정해!

250
Get me John. I need to speak to him.
존을 바꿔주세요. 얘기 좀 해야 돼요.

Get me sb …을 전화연결해줘, …을 데려와, 찾아와

251
Get off me, you freak!
꺼져, 이 괴짜야!

a freak 괴짜 **control freak** 통제광

252
Get over here! I need to talk to you.
이리와! 너랑 얘기해야 돼.

get over (to+장소) …로 오다

253
Get over yourself!
작작 좀 해라!, 주제파악 좀 해라!

254
Get the fuck out of my apartment!
내 아파트에서 당장 꺼지라고!

Get the fuck out! 꺼져버려!

255
Give it a try!
한번 해봐!

256
Give it to me straight.
솔직하게 말해줘.

257
Give me a break. I haven't done this before.
좀 봐줘요. 이런 적 처음이잖아요.

give sb a break 사정 좀 봐주다, 그만하다 = give it a break[rest]

258
Give me a call.
전화해.

259
Give me a chance. You'll see.
기회를 한번 줘. 두고 봐.

You'll see 곧 알게 될거야, 두고 보면 알아

260
Give me an hour or so, I'll see what I can do.
한 시간 정도만 줘봐, 내가 어떻게 해볼게.

I'll see what I can do 어떻게 해볼게 = Let me see what I can do

261
Give me some time to take it all in.
자세히 들여다보게 시간 좀 줘.

take it all in 천천히 하다, 자세히 보다

262
Give me strength to get through this ordeal.
이 시련을 극복할 힘을 주세요.

Give me strength! 더는 못참겠어!, …할 힘을 주세요(~ to+V)

263
Give me Tim.
팀 바꿔주세요.

Give me sb의 경우에는 전화에만 쓰이는데 반해 Get me sb하면 전화뿐만 아니라 「…을 데려오라」는 뜻으로도 쓰인다는 점을 기억해둔다.

264
Glad to get that off my chest. Thank you.
속에 있는 걸 털어놔서 기뻐. 고마워.

get ~ off one's chest 가슴 속에 있는 것을 털어놓다

265
Go ahead and let yourself out.
어서 알아서 나가.

show oneself out 알아서 혼자 나가다 let oneself in[out] 알아서 혼자 들어오다[나가다]

266
Go ahead with the festival preparation.
축제 준비를 계속해.

Go ahead with~ …을 계속하다

267
Go ahead! It won't hurt to try.
해봐! 손해 볼 것 없잖아.

not hurt to try 해봐도 손해볼게 없어

268
Go away! I don't want to see anybody.
가! 아무도 보고 싶지 않아.

Go away! 나가!, 꺼져!(Get out!)

269
Go easy on me. This is my first time.
살살해 줘. 나 처음이거든.

go easy on sb …을 봐주다 mercy 자비

270

Go easy, Sam. You didn't even know her.
천천히 하자고, 샘. 넌 아직 걜 알지도 못하잖아.
Go easy 진정해, 살살해 = Easy, easy

271

Go for it. You've got nothing to lose.
한번 해봐. 밑져야 본전이지.
You've got nothing to lose 밑져야 본전이야

272

Go get some rest.
가서 좀 쉬어.

273

Go nuts. It's really nice to sit in the warm water.
실컷 즐겨. 따뜻한 물에 앉아있는 건 정말 좋아.
Go nuts! 실컷 놀아봐!, 어서 해봐!

274

Go on, Tony! Give it to her!
계속해, 토니! 걔한테 더 해줘!
Give it to me! 섹스할 때 더 해줘!

275

God knows what he did to my daughter.
걔가 내 딸에게 무슨 짓했는지 아무도 몰라.
God knows(~)? 누가 알겠어? God knows that S+V 정말이지 …하다

276

Good for you. I hope you become a successful lawyer. 잘됐네. 네가 훌륭한 변호사가 되기를 바래.

Good for you 잘됐네

277

Good job, you were great!
잘했어, 넌 대단했어!

Good job! 잘했어 = Good work! = Good move!

278

Good Luck, I hope I'm wrong about you.
행운을 빌어, 너에 대한 나의 생각이 틀리기를 바래.

be right[wrong] about~ …에 대해 맞다[틀리다]

279

Good seeing you guys. Have fun.
만나서 반가웠어. 재밌게 보내.

have fun (with sb) (…와 함께) 재미있게 보내다 Have fun! 재미있게 보내!

280

Good to have you back.
너와 다시 함께 해서 좋아.

have sb (back) …와 (다시) 함께 하다, 불러주다

281

Got a sec? We need to discuss the schedule.
시간 돼? 일정 논의 좀 해야 돼.

(You) Got a minute[second]? 잠깐 시간 돼?

282

Got it. We'll be right down.
알았어. 금방 내려갈게.

I got it은 "이해했어," "알겠어," "물건을 샀어," "처리하다" 등의 뜻으로 쓰인다.

283

Gotta leave first in the morning.
낼 아침 일찍 가야 돼.

Gotta leave 나 가야 돼

284

Guess what? Chris and Sam are going to get married.
저기 말야. 크리스와 샘이 결혼할거래.

Guess what? 저기, 있잖아

285

Guys, come on, break it up guys!
야, 친구들, 그만 싸워!

break it up 싸움을 그만두다

SCREEN TIPS

사람을 부르는 호칭들.

친한 친구 사이거나 혹은 연인 사이에서
- **sweetheart, sweetie, honey[hon], babe, (my) dear**

남자친구들 사이에서 「어이!」,「야!」정도의 느낌
- **dude, buddy, bro, pal, man, guy** (여자들끼리는 girl을 사용)
- **boy** (얘야 – 나이어린 손아랫사람에게)
- **kiddo** 아이, 녀석   • **chap** 녀석, 친구

여러 명을 뭉뚱그려 말할 때
- **(you) guys** (얘들아 – 남녀 구분없이 사용하며, 손윗사람들을 향한 표현은 아님)

기타
- **hip** 최신 유행에 밝은 사람, 세련된 사람
- **buff** …광   • **roomie** 룸메이트
- **sport** 단짝 친구(chum), 또는 성격 좋은 사람
- **old man** 아버지, 남편, 직장상사

286

Hands off my woman.

내 여자에게서 손 떼.

hands off~ …에게서 손을 떼다, 건드리지 않다

287

Hard to believe he's such a fail.

걔가 그렇게 실패하다니 믿기 어렵구만.

be a fail 실수야, 잘못이야

288

Hard work's paying off. Keep up the good work. 열심히 일하면 보답이 오지. 지금처럼 계속 열심히 해.

Keep up the good work 계속 열심히 해

289

Have it your way.

네 맘대로 해, 좋을 대로 해.

290
Have you done anything to make money?
돈을 벌기 위해서 뭐라도 좀 해봤어?

make a buck[make a few bucks] 돈을 벌다 = make money

291
Have you gone mad?
너 제정신이야?

go mad 화내다(get angry), 사족을 못쓰다

292
Have you heard what he's been up to lately?
걔 최근에 어떻게 지내는지 들었어?

What have you been up to? 어떻게 지냈어?

293
Have you slept? You look like crap.
잠은 잤니? 너 엉망이야.

crap 헛소리, 엉망

294
Have you worked here long?
여기서 근무한지 오래됐어?

have worked~ 얼마동안 일하고 있다

295
Haven't we met before? Do you happen to know about Jane? **우리 만난 적 있나요? 혹시 제인 알아요?**

Haven't we met before? 우리 전에 만난 적 있나요?

296
Having a good day at work?
직장에서 잘 보내고 있어?

have a good day 좋은 하루를 보내다

297
Having a job is not all it's cracked up to be.
직장다니는게 다 그런 건 아냐.

be not all it's cracked up to be 사람들이 말하는 것과 다르다, 그런게 아니다

298
He always rambles when he's been drinking.
걘 술마시면 항상 횡설수설이야.

ramble 두서없이 횡설수설하다

299
He always seemed to have time on his hands.
걘 언제나 시간이 많은 것처럼 보였어.

have time on one's hand 시간이 남아돌다

300
He called off the wedding, and that was that.
걔가 결혼식을 취소했어, 일이 그렇게 된거야.

Is that it? 그런거야?, 내 말이 맞는거지?   That was that 일이 그렇게 된거야

301
He can't get enough of it.
걘 질리지가 않은 가봐.

can't get enough of sth …는 싫증나지 않아, 정말 최고야

302
He cheated on you, but you stayed friends?
너 몰래 바람피웠는데 친구로 남기로 했다고?
cheat on A (with B) A몰래 B와 바람피다

303
He completely goes to pieces.
걘 완전히 망가지고 있어.
go to pieces 엉망이 되다

304
He didn't even stick up for me.
걔는 내 편을 들어주지도 않았어.

305
He dislikes her, not the other way around.
걔는 그녀를 싫어해, 좋아하는게 아니고.
It was the other way around 정반대야

306
He drank a bottle of whiskey. What was he thinking?
위스키 한병을 다 마셨어. 무슨 생각으로 그랬대?
What was he thinking? 걘 무슨 생각으로 그런거야?

307
He flew into a rage and threw a chair.
걘 화를 버럭내고 의자를 집어 던졌어.
fly into a rage 버럭 화를 내다 get snaky 화를 내다

308

He goes out of his way to help me.
그는 날 돕기 위해 애를 많이 써.

go out of one's way to+V 애를 써서 …하다

309

He got worked up.
걔 열 받았어, 걔 대단했어.

310

He had this female boss. Real ball-buster, you know?
걘 이 여자가 보스래. 진짜 깐깐한 여자래, 알지?

ball-buster 엄한 사람, 엄한 상사

311

He has always had a weakness for chocolate.
걘 초콜릿하면 늘상 사족을 못써.

have a weakness for~ …에 약하다, 사족을 못쓰다, 좋아하다

312

He has to fight his way back from rock bottom.
걘 바닥에서 다시 일어나 싸워 나아가야 해.

fight one's way 싸워가며 나아가다

313

He has to lose some weight.
걘 살을 좀 빼야 돼.

put on weight 살이 찌다(⇔ lose one's weight 살이 빠지다)

314
He is being bullied at that school.
걘 학교에서 괴롭힘을 당하고 있어.

bully sb 괴롭히다

315
He is smart and funny, d'you ever think that about him?
걘 똑똑하고 재밌잖아. 그런 생각해본 적 없니?

316
He is still unaccounted for.
걔는 아직도 행방불명이야.

unaccounted for 행방불명의

317
He jerked off before you got there.
걘 네가 거기 도착하기 전에 자위했어.

jerk off 자위하다 = beat off, yank off, jack off, whack off

318
He just popped into my head.
불쑥 그의 생각이 났어.

pop into one's head 불쑥 …가 생각나다

319
He lashed out at everyone in the office.
걘 사무실의 모든 사람에게 화를 냈어.

lash out 화내다, 비난하다 wig sb out 분통을 터트리다

320
He mentioned in passing that he's seen you.
걔는 너를 봤다고 무심결에 말했어.

mention in passing 무심코 말하다, 나온 김에 말하다

321
He never called. I'm left hanging.
걔는 한번도 전화안했어. 나 혼자 남겨졌어.

leave sb hanging은 「…에게 알리지 않다」, 「기다리게 하다」라는 의미로 be left hanging하게 되면 「혼자 남게되다」라는 뜻.

322
He never got his courage up to ask her out.
걘 그녀에게 데이트 신청할 용기를 전혀 내지 못했어.

get courage up to+V 용기를 내서 …하다 = pluck up courage to+V

323
He never, ever saw it coming at all.
걘 그럴 줄 전혀 몰랐어.

see it[that] coming 어려운 상황이 될 줄 알다

324
He said he couldn't keep his eyes off me.
걘 내게서 눈을 뗄 수가 없다고 말했어.

can't take one's eyes off sb …에 눈을 떼지 못하다

325
He said it never happened before.
걔는 이런 적 한번도 없었다고 했어.

It never happened 전혀 그런 적 없어

326
He set me up.
걔가 날 속였어, 함정에 빠졌어.

set sb up …을 속이다

327
He takes a bite out of the sandwich.
걔는 샌드위치를 한입 먹고 있어.

take[have, get] a bite out of~ …을 한입 베어먹다

328
He takes pride in his work.
걘 자기 일에 자부심을 느끼는 것 같아.

take pride in~ …에 자부심을 느끼다

329
He told me that he's crazy about you.
걔가 나한테 말했는데 너한테 빠졌대.

be crazy about sb …에 빠지다   be crazy about sth …에 빠지다, 열성이다

330
He took one for the team!
걘 팀을 위해 총대를 맸어!

take one for the team 팀(전체)을 위해 나서다, 희생하다

331
He tries to get the best out of all of us.
걘 우리 모두를 최대한 활용하려고 하고 있어.

get the best out of~ …을 최대한 활용하다

332
He wants to set you up with his brother.
갠 너를 자기 형에게 소개시켜주고 싶어해.

set sb up with~ …을 …에게 소개시켜주다

333
He was head over heels about her.
갠 그녀에게 푹 빠져있었어.

be[fall] head over heels about sb …에게 홀딱 반하다

334
He was on his knees saying he was sorry.
갠 무릎을 꿇고 미안하다고 말하고 있었어.

be on one's knees 무릎을 꿇다

335
He was taken by surprise.
걔는 깜짝 놀랐어, 걔는 예상도 못했어.

336
He was told to leave after he bullocksed up at work.
갠 직장에서 엉망이 된 후 나가라는 말을 들었어.

bullocks up at work 직장에서 엉망이 되다

337
He went to the casino hoping to hit the jackpot.
갠 대박 터질 희망을 갖고 카지노에 갔어.

We hit the jackpot 땡 잡았다(We made a lot of money)

338
He won't take my calls.
내 전화를 안 받으려고 해.

take one's call …의 전화를 받다

339
He worked out his frustration.
걘 그의 좌절을 극복했어.

sb work (sth) out 문제를 해결하다

340
He'd never truly be happy until the day he met "the one." 걘 자기 짝을 만나는 날까지 절대로 행복해질 수 없을거야.

meet the one 천생연분을 만나다, 자기 짝을 만나다

341
He'd tell me to go with my gut.
걘 나보고 직감대로 행동하라고 말할거야.

go with one's gut 직감대로 행동하다

342
He'll be back, you'd better believe it.
걘 돌아올거야, 정말이야.

You'd better believe it 틀림없어, 정말이야

343
He'll never answer my calls.
걘 내 전화에 절대로 답하지 않을거야.

answer one's call …의 전화에 답하다 ring sb …에게 전화하다

344
He'll see it as a sign of relief.
걘 그걸 안도의 사인으로 볼거야.

see ~ as …을 …로 알다 see oneself as~ 스스로를 …로 생각하다

345
He's a little older, big deal, I mean, he's important to me.
그 남자 나이가 좀 많긴 하지만 별거 아냐, 내 말은 나한테 소중한 사람이니까.

346
He's been trying to screw her for months.
오랫동안 걔하고 섹스하려고 하고 있어.

screw (sb) …와 섹스하다 screw one's brains out 죽도록 섹스를 하다

347
He's girding his loins for the soccer match.
축구경기를 대비해서 긴장을 하고 있어.

gird one's loins 허리띠를 매다, 긴장하다

348
He's going out with Jane.
그 사람은 제인하고 사귀는 중야.

go out with sb …와 사귀다

349
He's gonna ride my ass for the rest of my life.
걘 평생 날 힘들게 할거야.

350
He's handsome and he went to Princeton.
걔는 잘 생겼고 프린스턴대 나왔대.

went to college 대학교에 진학하다, …학교를 나왔다

351
He's handsome and rich and I can't compete with that.
걘 잘생겼고 부자야, 난 도저히 못당하겠어.

I can't compete (with that) 도저히 못 당하겠군

352
He's having a lover's spat with Julie.
걘 줄리랑 사랑싸움을 하고 있어.

have a lover's spat with sb …와 사랑싸움하다 *spat 옥신각신, 입씨름

353
He's lying. That's what I was thinking.
걔는 거짓말하고 있어. 그게 바로 내가 생각하고 있던거야.

That's what I was thinking 이게 바로 내가 생각하고 있던거야

354
He's my steady.
쟤가 내가 사귀는 남자야.

be one's steady 오랫동안 사귀는 친구이다

355
He's not exactly nervous about tying the knot.
걘 결혼 땜에 초조한 건 아냐.

tie the knot (밧줄로 묶다) 결혼하다

356
He's not in his right mind.
그는 제정신이 아냐.

be not in one's right mind 제정신이 아니다, 미치다

357
He's off the hook.
걔 무사히 넘어갔어, 걔 무사해, (상황을) 무사히 넘겼어.

be off the hook 곤란한 상황을 벗어나다, 무사히 넘기다

358
He's over the moon that she accepted his proposal.
그녀가 청혼을 받아들여서 걔는 무척 기뻐하고 있어.

be over the moon 무척 기쁘다　be light on one's feet 날렵한, 춤을 잘 추는

359
He's picking up the pieces.
걔 재기 중이야.

pick up the pieces 재기하다, (몸, 마음) 추스리다

360
He's really stuck up!
걔는 정말 건방져!

be stuck up 거만하다

361
He's shagging his secretary.
걔는 비서와 잠자리를 해.

362

He's the spitting image of his father.
걘 아버지를 꼭 빼닮았어.

be the spitting image of~ …을 꼭 빼닮다

363

Heads up. Watch your back.
조심하고. 뒤를 잘 봐.

Watch your back! 조심해!

364

Hear me out. This is important.
내 말 좀 끝까지 들어봐. 중요한 문제라고.

Hear me out 내 말 끝까지 들어봐

365

Heard you got a new job. That going well?
새로 직장을 잡았다며. 그거 잘 돼가?

That going well? 그거 잘 돼가? = Is it going well?

366

Her career is going up in smoke.
걔의 경력은 다 수포로 돌아갔어.

go up in smoke 실패하다 shit the bed 실패하다

367

Her joke went too far.
걔 농담은 지나쳤어.

It's too far 너무 심했어 = be (totally) too much for sb = go too far

> 368

Here goes.
한번 해봐야지, 자 간다, 자 내가 먼저 한다.

> 369

Here I am Bridget Jones, one day short of 43.
여기 제가 브리짓 존스예요, 하루만 지나면 43살이 되죠.

short of~ 부족한…

> 370

Here it comes.
자 여기 있어, 잔소리에 또 시작이군.

> 371

Here it goes.
자, 시작하자.

> 372

Here it is.
(이야기를 건넬 때) 내 말을 들어봐.

> 373

Here they come. I say we make a break for it.
저기 걔네들이 와. 우리 도망쳐야 돼.

make a break for it 필사적으로 달아나다, 도망가다

374
Here we are.
자 (드디어) 도착했다, 뭔가 건네주면서 여기 있다.

375
Here we go again.
(상대방의 행동에) 또 시작하는구만.

376
Here we go.
자 간다, 여기 있다, 자 이제 시작해볼까.

377
Here you are.
(물건을 건네주면서) 자 여기 있어.

378
Here you go/ Here it is.
(물건 등을 건네며) 자, 여기 있어.

379
Here's ten dollars. That's all I got.
여기 10달러. 그게 가진거 전부야.

That's all I got 이게 전부 다야

380

Here's the deal. I need information.
거래하자. 난 정보가 필요해.

Here's the deal 좋은 생각이 있어, 이렇게 하자, 거래를 하자

381

Here's the opportunity I've always been looking for. 내가 계속 찾던 기회가 여기 있어.

have the opportunity to~ …할 기회가 있다

382

Here's the thing. I really like you.
내 말은 말야. 난 정말 네가 좋다구.

Here's the thing 내가 말하려는 건, 실은 말야

383

Here's to you.
당신을 위해 건배!, 너한테 주는 선물이야.

384

Here's what I want you to say.
이게 네가 말하기를 바라는거야.

385

Here's what I was thinking. Everyone needs more sleep. 이게 바로 내가 생각했던거야. 다들 잠을 더 자야 돼.

Here's what I was thinking 이게 바로 내가 생각했던거야

386

He's coming over tonight to help me put together my new furniture.

걔가 오늘밤에 와서 날 도와 새 가구를 조립할거야.

put together 한데 모으다, 조립하다, 준비하다

387

High profits are the beauty of the business.

고수익이 그 사업의 장점이야.

be the beauty of sth …의 장점이다

388

His landlord is such a d-bag.

걔 집주인은 정말이지 얼간이야.

d-bag(douchebag) 주로 불쾌한 남자

389

His love of his job is second only to his love of family. 걔는 일에 대한 사랑이 가족애 빼면 첫째야.

be second only to~ …빼면 첫째다, …에 버금가다

390

His Portuguese is really coming on.

걔의 포르투갈어는 정말 발전하고 있어.

come on (with) 발전하다, 진전하다 나아지다

391
Hit me up anytime.
언제든 연락해.
hit sb up 연락하다, 만나다

392
Hold on a second! I don't work for you!
잠깐만! 난 네 밑에서 일 안해!
Hold on (a second, moment, minute) 잠시만

393
Hold your horses.
서두르지마.

394
Hoping a hot bath will do the trick.
뜨겁게 목욕하면 효과가 있을거야.
do the trick 효과가 있다

395
How 'bout you come back here on your day off? 쉬는 날 이리로 돌아오는게 어때?

396
How about I give you a ride home?
내가 집까지 데려다 줄까?
give sb a ride[lift] …을 차 태워주다   get a ride[lift] 차를 얻어타다

397

How about we send out a holiday card this year? 함께 크리스마스 카드를 보내는게 어때?

398

How about you? Are you seeing anyone?

넌 어때? 누구 만나는 사람있어?

How about you? 네 생각은 어때? = What about you?

399

How are you doing on the report you're writing? 네가 쓰고 있는 보고서 어떻게 하고 있어?

How are you doing with[on]~? …은 어떻게 돼가?

400

How are you doing? It's been a while.

잘 지냈어? 오랜만이야.

How (are) you doing? 잘 지내?, 괜찮아? How are you? 잘 지내?, 괜찮아?

401

How can I tell?

내가 어찌 알아?

402

How could she pull a stunt like this?

어떻게 걔가 이런 바보 같은 짓을 할 수 있을까?

pull that stunt 바보 같은 짓을 하다 hit a wall 난관에 부딪히다

403
How could this happen?
어떻게 이럴 수가 있어?, 이런 일이 있을 수가?

404
How could you do this[that]?
어쩜 그럴 수가 있니?

405
How could you not know that? You call yourself a writer. 어떻게 저걸 모를 수가 있어? 자칭 작가라는 작자가.

You call yourself~ 소위 …라는 사람이

406
How dare you! I'm a married man!
네가 뭔데 그래! 난 유부남이야!

How dare you! 네가 감히! How dare you+V! 어떻게 감히 …할 수가 있어!

407
How did it go with Joshua last night?
지난밤에 조슈아하고는 어떻게 됐어?

How did it go with sb? …하고는 어떻게 됐어?

408
How did you even call him?
어떻게 그 사람한테 전화까지 한거냐구?

409
How did you think that was gonna come up?
어떻게 그런 얘기가 나오겠어?

come up 논의되다, 언급되다

410
How do I go about seducing a woman who is apparently out of my league?
내가 어떻게 나한테 과분한 상대인 여자를 유혹하겠어?

be out of one's league 상대가 안되다, 과분한 상대이다

411
How do you fancy stretching the night out a bit?
어떻게 밤 늦게 더 노는게 어때?

fancy ~ing …하는 것을 좋아하다

412
How do you feel about the two of us having a baby together? 우리 함께 애기 갖는거 어떻게 생각해?

How do you feel about~? …에 대해서 어떻게 생각해?

413
How fast can you make it happen?
얼마나 빨리 그걸 할 수 있어?

make it happen 그렇게 되도록 하다, 성공하다

414
How have you been? You look great!
어떻게 지냈니? 근사해 보이는데!

How have you been? 어떻게 지냈어?

415

How long has he been like this?
걔가 얼마나 이런 상태였던거야?

be (usually) like this[that] 보통 이렇다

416

How long have you been in love with Chris?
크리스와 사랑한지 얼마나 됐어?

be in love with sb …을 사랑하고 있다

417

How many more boxes would you have to sell in order to win?
이기려면 몇상자나 더 팔아야 하는거죠?

418

How many times do I have to say I'm sorry?
내가 미안하다고 몇번이나 말해야 돼?

419

How many times do I have to tell you?
도대체 몇 번을 말해야 알겠어?

420

How much do I owe you?
내가 얼마를 내면 되지?, 얼마죠?

421
How often do you text message your friends?
친구들에게 얼마나 자주 문자를 보내?

text (message) 문자, 문자를 보내다

422
How should I know?
내가 어떻게 알아?, 난 전혀 몰라, 난들 어찌 알겠어?

423
How would that be?
그러면 어떨까?, 그러면 좋겠어?

424
How would you know, were you here?
네가 어떻게 알겠어, 여기 있었어?

How would you know that? 네가 그걸 어떻게 알겠어?

425
How would you like me to take you out to a fancy restaurant? **내가 고급식당에 데려가는거 어때?**

take sb out to~ …을 데리고 …로 나가다

426
How'd the audition go?
오디션은 어떻게 됐어?

How did sth go? …는 어떻게 됐어?

427
How'd you get so good at teaching?
어떻게 그렇게 잘 가르치게 됐어요?

get good[poor] at~ …을 잘 [못]하다

428
How're things working out with her?
걔하고는 일이 어떻게 돼가고 있어?

work out with sb 상황 등이 돌아가다

429
How's it going with the wedding?
결혼은 어떻게 돼가?

How's it going with sth? …은 어떻게 돼가?

430
How's it going? How you holding up?
어떻게 지내? 어떻게 버티고 있는거야?

How's it going? 어떻게 지내?, 잘 지내?

431
How's that working out for you?
그러니까 어때?, 너한테 잘 되어가니?

work out 잘 되어가다

432
How's your new job going?
요즘 새로운 일은 어때?

How's everything going? 다 잘 돼가?

Check it Out!
문장속에서 확인해보기!

A: Got a minute to review the notes from the meeting?
B: Sure, let's go to my office and <u>take a look at</u> them.

take a look at~
look at~이라고 동사로 쓸 수도 있지만, 동사(look)의 동일한 형태의 명사형을 써서 take a look at~이란 형태를 선호하는 경우가 많다.

A: 회의에서 나온 사항을 검토할 시간 있으세요?
B: 물론이죠. 내 사무실로 가서 한번 봅시다.

A: How is it coming? Are you finished hook<u>ing</u> up the Internet on my computer?
B: All set. Try it now.

be finished~ing
be finished는 끝내다라는 뜻. 동일한 의미인 하지만 더 캐주얼한 be done~ 역시 바로 ~ing가 와서 …을 끝내다라는 뜻으로 쓰인다.

A: 어떻게 돼가요? 인터넷 연결 끝났어요?
B: 다 됐어요. 이제 해보세요.

A: Well, I'm gonna get another espresso. **Can I get you something?**
B: Thanks. I'll have <u>a cup of coffee</u> and a muffin.

a cup of coffee
커피는 확실히 셀 수 없는 명사이기 때문에 a cup of~를 써서 양을 말하는게 맞지만 보통 한잔씩 팔고 또 그렇게 들고다니기 때문에 a coffee라고 마치 셀 수 있는 명사처럼 쓰이기도 한다.

A: 음, 난 에스프레소 한 잔 더 마셔야겠다. 뭐 좀 사다줄까?
B: 고마워. 그럼 커피 한 잔하고 머핀 하나 먹을래.

A: Jack, you helped us make a huge profit. **Here's to you.**
B: Thanks boss. I feel really happy to be employed by our company.

help+사람+동사
help는 사역동사 일원으로 help+사람~ 다음에 'to'없는 동사원형을 쓴다. 물론 예전에는 'to'를 쓰기도 했으나 최근 추세는 안쓰는 경향이 뚜렷하다.

A: 잭, 자네 덕분에 큰 이익을 냈어. 자 받게.
B: 감사합니다 사장님. 우리 회사에서 일하고 있다는게 정말 기쁩니다.

A: I really wish you wouldn't drive so fast. It's dangerous.
B: **Give me a break.** You were driving a lot faster than me a little while ago!

I hope S+V vs. I wish S+V
I hope~는 현실적 가능성이 있는 것으로 종속절 시제는 현재형. I wish~는 현실과 가능성이 없어보이는. 즉 현실과 반대되는 내용을 언급할 때 사용하고 시제 또한 과거형을 쓴다는 점이 다르다.

A: 너무 속력을 내지 말았으면 정말 좋겠어. 위험하잖아.
B: 무슨 소리야. 얼마 전까지만 해도 나보다 훨씬 속도를 냈으면서!

A: I am going to have to punish Kelly. She's been very bad lately.
B: **Go easy on her.** She's a good kid. She'll behave if we just talk to her.

She's been very bad lately
현재완료는 과거부터 현재까지 이어지는 특이한 시제로 특정 시점(an hour ago)이나 기간(for a week)을 나타내는 부사구와는 쓰이지 않는다.

A: 켈리한테 벌을 줘야겠어. 요즘 버릇이 아주 나빠.
B: 살살 해. 착한 애잖아. 말로 타이르면 얌전하게 굴거야.

후다닥 스크린영어
대표문장 2500

001
I admit it, I am in the wrong about the rules.
내가 인정할게, 내가 규칙을 어겼어.
I admit it 내가 인정할게

002
I almost didn't make it to the party.
그 파티에 못 갈 뻔했어.
make it (to~) …에 도착하다

003
I always like to start off with a hug.
난 항상 껴안는 것으로 시작하길 좋아해.
to start off 우선 start off with …로 시작하다

004
I am aware of what goes on in my own house.
내 집에서 무슨 일이 벌어지는지 잘 알고 있지.
I'm aware of what~ …을 알고 있어

005
I am glad to be here. I have had a rough day.
여기 있어서 너무 좋아. 정말 힘든 하루였어.

have a rough day 힘든 하루를 보내다

006
I am nobody's fool.
날 물로 보지마.

007
I am not letting him slip away.
난 걔가 몰래 떠나지 못하도록 할거야.

slip away 몰래 빠져나가다

008
I am not on board with this!
난 이것에 동참할 수 없어!

be on board 탑승하다, 조직[회사]에서 함께 일하다

009
I am not sure that you and Olivia really mesh well together. 너와 올리비아가 잘 맞는지 잘 모르겠어.

mesh well together 죽이 잘맞다 = hit it off = be a big hit with sb

010
I am nuts[mad] about you.
난 널 열렬히 좋아해.

go[be] nuts for[over, about] 열광하다, 몰입하다 = be crazy[mad] for[about]

011
I am serious. I mean it.
장난아냐. 진심이야.

I mean it 진심이야

012
I am sick of this.
진절머리가 나.

be sick of~ …가 진절머리 나다

013
I am single as fuck.
난 정말 독신이구나.

as fuck 아주, fuck-all = nothing

014
I am so busted.
딱 걸렸네, 나 큰일났네.

bust 깨부수다, 체포하다, (경찰이) 쳐들어오다, 들키다

015
I am sorry to hear that.
안됐네.

016
I am sorry you had to go through it.
그 일을 겪어야 했다니 안됐네.

Sorry you had to see that 이런 모습 보게 해서 미안해

017
I am totally burned out.
완전히 뻗었어.

be burned out 다 소진되다, 녹초가 되다

018
I am very appreciative of what you've done.
해주신 일 정말 감사해요.

be appreciative of~ …가 고마워

019
I appreciate you driving Jack home.
차로 잭을 집에 데려다줘서 정말 고마워.

I appreciate+N …가 고마워 I appreciate you ~ing …해줘서 고마워

020
I asked you to watch your language.
말조심하라고 말했잖아.

watch one's language 말조심하다

021
I beg to differ. I'm five weeks older than you.
난 생각이 달라. 내가 너보다 5주 나이가 많아.

beg to differ 생각이 다르다

022
I beg your pardon? Could you repeat that?
뭐라구요? 다시 말해줄래요?

I beg your pardon? 다시 말해주세요

023
I begged him not to leave. We made love that night. 난 걔한테 떠나지 말라고 간청했어. 그날 우린 사랑을 나눴어.

make love 사랑을 나누다, 섹스하다

024
I believe he's taken.
난 그가 유부남이라고 믿고 있어.

be taken 임자 있는 몸이다

025
I blew it.
망쳤어, 기회를 날려버렸어.

blow it 부주의나 실수로 기회를 놓치다

026
I called your cell like a zillion times.
네 핸드폰으로 수없이 전화했었어.

call one's cell …의 핸드폰으로 전화를 하다

027
I came across one of his baby pictures last weekend. 지난 주에 걔의 어렸을 적 사진을 우연히 봤어.

come across sb[sth] 우연히 만나다

028
I came back to check on him to see if he was okay. 난 걔가 괜찮은지 확인하려고 걔를 살펴보러 돌아왔어.

check on sb[sth] 확인해보다

029
I can get it done in a flash.
그거 순식간에 끝낼 수 있어.

in a flash 순식간에(like a flash)

030
I can help you carry those bags. Let me.
그 가방 드는거 도와드릴게요. 제가 할게요.

좀 쓰다만 표현 같지만 Let me는 상대방이 하는 일을 도와주겠다고 적극 나서면서 하는 말이다.

031
I can kick the crap out of him.
걔를 열나게 패줄 수 있어.

kick the shit[crap] out of sb 흠씬 패주다   get the shit[crap] kicked out of sb 흠씬 얻어맞다

032
I can live with that.
괜찮아, 참을 만해.

can live with that 견딜만하다, 괜찮다

033
I can put you up for a while.
잠시 집에 머물게 해줄 수 있어.

put sb up 집에 머물게 하다, 재워주다

034
I can see that Jack has a new suit.
잭이 새로운 옷을 입었네.

I can see that 알겠어, 알고 있어, 알아

035
I can swing by on Sunday and pick you up?
내가 일요일에 들러서 널 픽업할까?

swing by 잠시 들르다 = run by

036
I can take it if it's that.
그게 그렇다면 받아들일 수 있다.

037
I can't believe he's dating that slut in marketing!
걔가 마케팅 부서의 그 헤픈 여자랑 사귀다니 믿을 수가 없어!

038
I can't believe how much I love her, I can't get enough of her.
난 그녀를 너무 사랑해. 그녀는 전혀 싫증이 나지 않아.

Can't get enough of sb …는 싫증나지 않아, 정말 최고야

039
I can't believe I forgot this.
이걸 잊을 줄은 차마 몰랐네.

040
I can't believe she left me.
걔가 날 떠나다니.

I can't believe it 이럴 수가, 그럴 리가   I can't believe S+V …하다니

041
I can't complain.
잘 지내.

042
I can't get into that right now.
나중에 이야기하자.

043
I can't help it. He gives me the creeps.
어쩔 수 없어. 걔를 보면 섬뜩한 느낌이 든다구.

044
I can't let her get to me.
걔한테 괴롭힘을 당하지 않을거야.

get to sb 연락이 닿다, 괴롭히거나 힘들게 하다

045
I can't let this happen.
그렇게 되도록 두지 않겠어.

not let sth happen 그렇게 되도록 두지 않다

046
I can't put up with this sort of shit.
난 이런 개떡 같은 것을 참을 수가 없어.

shit time 거지 같은 시간 **this sort of shit** 이런 개떡 같은 것

047
I can't take it anymore.
더 이상 못 견디겠어.

048
I can't thank you enough.
어떻게 감사해야 할지.

049
I could just eat her up.
잡아먹을 수 있을 정도로 매력적이다.

eat sb up …을 잡아먹을 정도로 매력적이다 Eat me 엿먹어, (여성)오랄섹스해줘

050
I could use a little help here.
여기 좀 도와줬으면 해.

could use+N …가 있었으면 좋겠다, …이 필요하다

051
I couldn't ask you to do that.
(고맙지만) 그러지 않아도 돼.

052
I couldn't care less.
알게 뭐람. (전혀 관심없다.)

053
I couldn't have said it better.
동감이야, 더 이상 어떻게 말을 해, 진짜야.

054
I couldn't keep a straight face.
웃음을 참을 수 없었어.

keep a straight face 웃지 않다, 진지한 표정을 짓다

055
I couldn't talk to him. He was wrecked.
걔와 얘기를 할 수 없었어. 엄청 취했거든.

be wrecked 맛이 가다, 취하다 get sloshed[shitfaced] 엄청 취하다

056
I did everything I could think of to save him.
난 그를 살리기 위해 최선을 다했어.

do one's best one can[could] 최선을 다하다 = do everything one could think of

057
I did it wrong.
내가 잘못했어, 내가 실수했어.

058
I did it!
해냈어!

059
I didn't know anything about this, I swear.
난 이거에 대해 전혀 몰라, 정말야.

I swear 정말이야, 맹세해 I swear to God 하늘에 두고 맹세코

060
I didn't know that.
전혀 몰랐었어, 몰랐네, 모르고 있었지 뭐야.

061
I didn't mean it. I was just joking with her.
고의로 그런 건 아냐. 그냥 걜 놀린 것 뿐인데.

I was just joking around 농담한거였어 joke with sb …을 놀리다

062
I didn't see that coming.
그럴 줄 몰랐어.

063
I do this all the time. It's easy for me.
내가 매일 하는 일이야. 나한테는 쉬운 일이야.

do this all the time 항상 이래

064
I don't believe it, but let's see what you get.
믿기지 않아, 하지만 어떻게 되나 보자고.

Let's see what you get 어떻게 되나 보자, 능력을 보여줘(Let me see what you got)

065
I don't blame you for being angry.

네가 화낼 만도 해.

I don't blame you for~ 네가 …할 만해

066
I don't blame you.

그럴 만도 해, 네가 어쩔 수 없었잖아.

067
I don't blame you. It was an accident.

그럴 수도 있지. 사고였는데.

068
I don't blame you. It's cold outside.

이해해, 그럴 만도 해.

069
I don't care who he sleeps with.

걔가 누구랑 자는지 관심없어.

I don't care (about~/what~/if~) 신경안써, 상관없어

070
I don't cry! It's not a big deal!

난 울지 않아! 별일도 아닌데!

071
I don't deserve such a good daughter.
난 그렇게 좋은 딸을 갖을 자격이 안돼.

deserve sth …을 누릴 자격이 있다

072
I don't ever want to see you again. Is that clear?
널 다신 보고 싶지 않아. 알겠어?

Is that clear? 내 말 알겠지?, 무슨 뜻인지 알겠지?

073
I don't feel like it.
됐어, 사양할래.

074
I don't feel right about dating someone else.
다른 사람과 데이트하는게 옳다고 생각하지 않아.

feel right about~ …에 대해 옳다고 생각하다

075
I don't get high.
난 약 안해.

get high 술, 마약에 취하다 drug high 마약에 흥분한 상태

076
I don't give a shit.
알게 뭐야.

077
I don't have time for this.
이럴 시간 없어.

078
I don't know about that.
글쎄.

079
I don't know how to put it.
그걸 어떻게 말해야 할지 모르겠어.

put it 표현하다 = express

080
I don't know how to tell you this, but your wife is in the hospital. 어떻게 말해야 할지 모르겠지만 네 아내가 병원에 있어.

I don't know how to tell you this, 어떻게 이걸 말해야 할지 모르겠지만,

081
I don't know if it's gonna fit in here.
이게 여기에 어울릴지 모르겠어.

I don't fit in here 난 여기에 안 어울려

082
I don't know if you are serious about dating me. 네가 나랑 진지하게 데이트를 하는 건지 모르겠어.

be[get] serious (about) 진지해지다, 심각해지다

083
I don't know what came over me.
내가 왜 그랬는지 모르겠어.

What's got into you? 도대체 왜 그러는거야?, Sth come over sb …가 …을 엄습하다

084
I don't know what else to do.
달리 어떻게 해야 할지 모르겠어.

085
I don't know what to say to her.
걔한테 뭐라고 말해야 할지 모르겠어.

I don't know what to say about[to]~ …에 대해 뭐라 말해야 할지

086
I don't know what to say. I'm disappointed in you, Jack.
뭐라 해야 할지. 잭, 네게 실망했어.

I don't know what to say 뭐라 말해야 할지

087
I don't know what you mean.
그게 무슨 말이야.

088
I don't know, really. Just killing time, I suppose.
난 모르겠어, 정말. 그냥 시간이나 보낼까봐.

I suppose 그런 것 같아

089
I don't know. I'll find out though.
몰라. 그렇지만 알아보려구.

090
I don't like to eat fish, apart from fried fish.
생선튀김을 제외하고 생선먹는 걸 좋아하지 않아.

apart from sth …을 제외하고, …뿐만 아니라

091
I don't micro-manage. I don't shy away from delegating.
난 세세하게 관리하지 않아. 주저없이 위임을 하지.

092
I don't remember how we ended up in bed together.
난 어떻게 우리가 함께 침대에 있게 되었는지 기억을 못해.

end up with[in] 결국 …한 상태가 되다 = end up ~ing

093
I don't see it that way.
난 그렇게 생각하지 않아, 그런 것 같지 않아.

094
I don't see why not.
그럼, 안 될 이유가 어딨어.

095
I don't see why not. Let's go get some ice cream. 그러지 뭐. 가서 아이스크림 좀 먹자.
I don't[see] why not 안될 것 뭐 있어?, 그러지 뭐

096
I don't think he'll make a move on me again.
걔가 다시 내게 집적댈거라고 생각안해.
make a move on sb …에 집적대다

097
I don't think she's up for anything.
걘 뭔가 할 준비가 안되어 있는 것 같아.
be up for sth …에 관심이나 의향이 있다

098
I don't think so. I heard it's so boring.
아닐 걸, 무척 재미없다고 하던데.
I think so 그럴 걸 I don't think so 그렇지 않을 걸

099
I don't think this can wait.
이건 미룰 수 없는거야.
This can wait 나중에 해도 돼 ⇔ That can't wait

100
I don't throw myself at guys.
난 남자들에게 들이대지 않아.
throw oneself at~ 들이대다

101
I don't want my daughter hanging around with a guy like that! 내 딸이 저런 자식과 어울리는게 싫어!

hang around (with sb) (…와 함께) 시간을 보내다

102
I don't want to get in the way.
방해하고 싶지 않아.

get[be] in the way 방해가 되다

103
I don't want to get into that right now.
지금 당장 그 문제를 얘기하고 싶지 않아.

Let's not get into that 그 얘기는 하지 말자

104
I don't want to leave you high and dry.
네가 힘든데 모른 척하기 싫어.

105
I don't want to mess you up.
난 너를 혼란스럽게 하고 싶지 않아.

mess sb up 혼란스럽게 하다, 어지럽게 하다

106
I don't want to wear out my welcome.
너무 실례되는게 아닌지 몰라.

wear out one's welcome 너무 오래 머물러 눈총받다(자신의 환영을 닳아 없어지게 한다는 의미)

107

I don't want you to get involved in my problem. 네가 내 문제에 연루되는 걸 원치 않아.

get[be] involved in[with]~ 연루되다, 관련되다

108

I doubt if Howard joined the gathering.
하워드가 모임에 함께 했다고 생각하지 않아.

I doubt if S+V …하지 않을거야

109

I doubt it. You haven't been a very good student. 그럴까? 그리 좋은 학생은 아니잖아.

I doubt it[that] 그렇지 않을거야

110

I doubt that's going to happen.
난 그런 일이 일어나지 않을 것 같아.

I doubt that S+V …하지 않을거야

111

I ended up getting married and having kids.
결혼도 하고 아이들도 낳게 됐어.

end up ~ing 결국 …하게 되다

112

I fancy one of those designer dresses.
저 디자이너 드레스들 중 하나를 갖고 싶어.

fancy sth 갖고 싶다, 좋아하다 = want to have or do something

113
I feel like I could go for three more.
3개 더 먹고 싶어.

I could go for sth …을 하고 싶어

114
I feel like I might bump into you.
우연히 당신과 부딪힐 것 같아요.

bump into sb[sth] 우연히 만나다

115
I feel like you are not listening to me.
네가 내 말을 듣지 않은 것 같아.

You're not listening to me 너 내 말 안듣는구나 Are you listening to me? 내 말 듣고 있어?

116
I feel terrible. I have to call in sick.
몸이 정말 안 좋아. 아파서 결근한다고 해야 되겠어.

call in sick 아파 출근 못한다고 전화하다

117
I fell for one chick and I'm losing my mind.
난 한 여자에게 푹 빠져서 제정신이 아냐.

lose one's mind 제정신이 아니다, 미치다

118
I forgot my money at home.
깜빡하고 돈을 집에 두고 왔네.

119

I get it. It was a stupid idea.

알겠어. 그건 어리석은 생각야.

I get it 이해가 되네 I get your drift 이해가 돼

120

I get that a lot.

그런 얘기 많이 들어.

121

I get that guys don't want to hang out with the girl with the boyfriend.

남자들은 남친이 있는 여자하고는 놀고 싶어하지 않아.

hang out with sb …와 함께 시간을 보내다, …와 함께 놀다

122

I get that you're mad. You deserve to be mad.

너 화난 것을 이해해. 너는 화가 날 만하지.

You deserve to+V …할 만하다

123

I get that. You should hang on to this.

알았어. 이거 놓치지 않는게 좋겠어.

hang on to~ 꽉 붙잡다, 놓치지 않다

124

I get the point. I won't do that.

알겠어. 안 그럴게.

I get the point 무슨 말인지 이해했어

125
I go crazy for it.
그 때문에 난 화가 나.

go crazy 무척 화를 내다, 열광하다, 열심히 …하다

126
I got a little tied up with work.
난 일하느라 좀 바빴어.

be tied up with~ …로 꼼짝달싹 못하다

127
I got a lot of heat for making a bad decision.
난 결정을 잘못해서 많은 비난을 받았어.

get a lot of heat 물이 오르다, 많은 비난을 받다

128
I got a phone call to make.
전화 한 통화하고.

make the call 전화를 하다

129
I got a question for you. Just a little thing, no pressure.
물어볼게 있어. 간단한거야, 스트레스 받지 말고.

No pressure 부담주려는 것은 아냐, 스트레스받지 말고

130
I got a thing about this.
난 이게 무척이나 좋아.

131
I got back in one piece.
무사히 돌아왔어.
in one piece 무사히, 온전히

132
I got held up at work.
직장에서 일에 잡혀있었어.

133
I got hooked on TV.
TV에 중독됐어.
get hooked on~ …에 중독되다

134
I got it. Go get some fresh air.
알았어. 가서 신선한 공기 좀 쐬라.
Some fresh air would do you good 바람 좀 쐬면 도움이 될거야

135
I got my heart set on it.
나 그거 하기로 했어.
have one's heart set on~ …을 하기로 맘먹다, (굳게) 결심하다

136
I got suckered into helping her move.
나 속아서 걔 이사하는거 도와줬어.
get suckered into 속아서 …하다

137
I got the impression she was going to meet someone. 걔가 누굴 만날거라는 인상을 받았어.

get the impression~ …라는 인상이나 느낌을 받다 give sb an impression 인상을 주다

138
I got this, and I'll take care of it.
내가 처리할게, 내가 알아서 처리할게.

I got this 내가 처리할게, 내가 낼게 = I can handle it

139
I got to run, and I ran into you.
서둘러가다 너를 우연히 만났어.

run into sb[sth] 우연히 만나다

140
I got your back.
내가 뒤를 봐줄게.

get sb's back …의 뒤를 봐주다, 도와주다

141
I got your cell. I'll be in touch.
네 핸드폰 받았어. 내가 연락할게.

get[be] in touch (with sb) 연락하다, 연락을 취하다

142
I gotta get going in a few minutes myself.
난 좀 후에 가봐야 돼.

I gotta get going 나 가봐야 돼 We should get going 우리 가봐야 돼

143
I gotta go. I'll talk to you soon.
전화끊어야 돼. 또 통화하자.

(I've) Gotta go 나 가야 돼, (전화) 끊을게

144
I gotta stop buying into the bullshit.
헛소리를 믿지 말아야되겠어.

buy into the bullshit 허튼 소리를 믿다

145
I guess I've gotten carried away.
너무 정신없이 내 얘기만 했네.

get carried away 몰입하다, …에 빠지다

146
I guess it's better to play it safe though.
그래도 안전하게 하는게 나을 것 같아.

play it safe 조심하다, 신중을 기하다

147
I had a crush on you when I first met you!
내가 널 첨 봤을 때 너한테 반했어!

have (got) a crush on sb …에 반하다 be sweet on …에 반하다

148
I had a lot of work to catch up on.
밀린 일이 아주 많아.

catch up on 밀린 것을 하다

149
I had no idea you are into this stuff.
네가 이런 걸 좋아하는지 몰랐어.
be into sth …에 푹 빠지다, 몰입하다

150
I hate myself for doing this.
이렇게 하고 싶지 않아.

151
I hate to break this up, but I have to go.
얘기 끊어서 미안하지만, 나 가야 돼.
I hate to break this up, 얘기 끊어서 미안하지만,

152
I hate you. You've ruined my life.
난 네가 싫어. 넌 내 인생을 망쳤어.
ruin one's life 인생을 망치다

153
I hate your guts.
정말 너 싫어.

154
I have a favor to ask you.
너에게 부탁할게 있는데.
ask sb a favor …에게 부탁하다

155
I have a feeling that John is going to quit his job.
존이 직장을 그만두려는 것 같아.

quit one's job 회사를 그만두다

156
I have a lot on my plate.
신경쓸게 많아, 할 일이 많아.

have a lot on one's plate 해야 할 일이 많다

157
I have a question for you.
질문 있는데, 물어볼게 있어.

158
I have a surprise for you.
너 놀래켜줄게 있어.

I have ~ for you 네게 줄 …가 있어   I have something for you 네게 줄게 있어

159
I have been friends with Chris since childhood.
크리스와는 어린 시절부터 친구로 지내고 있어.

be friends with~ …와 친구이다

160
I have been thinking of going elsewhere.
다른 곳으로 가는 걸 생각해왔어.

I've been thinking of ~ …을 생각 중이었어

161
I have got another call.
다른 전화가 와서.

162
I have never, ever scored a hot bartender.
섹시한 바텐더하고 절대 자본 적 없어.

score (with) sb 처음 본 …와 섹스하다

163
I have no clue what that means.
그게 무슨 의미인지 전혀 모르겠어.

Not a clue 전혀 몰라 not have a clue; have no clue 전혀 모르다

164
I have no excuse for not coming home yesterday. 어제 외박한거 변명할 말이 없어.

make an excuse 변명하다 have an[no] excuse 변명거리가 있다[없다]

165
I have no idea what you're talking about.
네가 무슨 말을 하는 건지 모르겠어.

I have no idea 모르겠어 You have no idea 넌 상상도 못할거야

166
I have no idea whose side you're on.
네가 누구 편인지 모르겠어.

be on one's side …의 편을 들다

167
I have nothing to do with this.
난 아무 관련이 없어.

168
I have nothing to say to you.
네게 아무 할 말이 없어.

I got nothing to say 할 말이 없네

169
I have some issues I need to work through.
내가 풀어야 하는 문제가 좀 있어.

I have issues 문제가 있어

170
I have the classic male problem of no follow-through. 난 애프터 신청을 하지 않는 전형적인 남자 기질이 있어요.

Classic sth 전형적인…

171
I have to say you really impressed me today.
오늘 너한테 정말 감동받았다고 말해야겠어.

I have to say S+V …라고 해야 되겠어

172
I have to set her free, let Mother Nature take its course. 난 그녀를 풀어주고 자연에 맡겨야 해.

let nature take its course 순리대로 하다

173
I have to take a minute to check it out.
잠깐 시간내서 그걸 확인해봐야겠어.

Sb take a second to+V 잠깐 시간내서 …하다

174
I have to tell you something. It's about your ex-wife. 말할게 있는데 네 전 부인 이야기야.

I have to tell you (something) (진지하게) 정말이지, 할 말이 있는데

175
I have[I've got] better things to do.
시간낭비야, 그걸 할 바에는 다른 걸 하겠어.

176
I haven't got all day.
빨리 좀 해줘, 내가 시간이 없어, 여기서 이럴 시간 없어.

177
I hear what you're saying. I'm with you.
무슨 말인지 알아. 동감야.

I'm with you (there) 동감야, 알았어

178
I hear what you're saying.
무슨 말인지 알겠어.

I hear[know] what you're saying 무슨 말인지 알겠어

179

I heard about it second hand.
전해 들었어.

180

I heard you hack computers. You any good?
컴퓨터 해킹을 한다고 들었는데, 그거 잘해?

You any good? 넌 뭐 좀 하냐?, (그거) 잘 해?

181

I hope you don't mind me calling you.
내가 네게 전화를 해도 괜찮기를 바래.

I hope you don't mind (~) (…해도) 괜찮겠지

182

I hope you know you still mean a lot to me.
아직 네가 내겐 큰 의미가 된다는 걸 알아주길 바래.

mean a lot to sb …에게 소중[중요]하다

183

I just can't get past it.
그걸 잊을 수가 없어, 아직도 못 잊겠어.

get past (sth[sth]) (…을) 잊다, …지나치다

184

I just feel kind of silly that I made such a big fuss about my ring.
반지 갖고 야단법석을 떨다니 내가 좀 어리석었어.

make a fuss about~ 불필요하게 야단법석을 떨다

185
I just got back on the market.
난 다시 이성을 구하고 있어.

get back on the market 다시 애인을 구하다

186
I just got my ass kicked for you.
너 때문에 아주 혼쭐났어.

kick one's ass 혼내다, 물리치다 get one's ass kicked 혼쭐나다

187
I just got off the phone with him.
나 걔와 방금 통화했는데.

get off the phone with sb …와 방금 통화하다

188
I just got that jerk out of my mind!
나 그 자식 잊어버렸어!

a jerk 바보, 멍충이

189
I just had time to pop in.
짬내서 잠깐 들렀어.

pop in 예고없이 잠깐 들르다

190
I just ran out of excuses.
이젠 변명거리도 다 떨어졌어.

run[be] out of excuses 변명거리가 떨어지다 run out of options 선택지가 줄다

> 191

I just spilt coffee on my new dress.
새 옷에 커피를 쏟았어.

> 192

I just wanna make up for it by taking you out shopping.
널 데리고 쇼핑하러 나가서 네 맘을 좀 풀어주고 싶어.

make up for (안좋은 일 등에 대해) 보상하다, 벌충하다

> 193

I just wanna make things work again.
난 단지 일이 다시 제대로 돌아가길 원해.

make things work 잘 돌아가게 하다

> 194

I just want to get it over with.
난 그냥 빨리 해치워버렸으면 좋겠어.

get over with~ 끝내다   get it over with 빨리 끝내버리다

> 195

I just want to get this incident behind me.
난 그냥 이번 일을 잊고 싶어.

get behind 늦다, 뒤지다, 지지하다, 잊다

> 196

I just wanted to follow up that text with a phone call.
문자보고 그냥 전화통화하고 싶었어.

follow up the text with a phone call 문자보고 전화하다

197
I just wanted to get away from the people I see all the time. 늘상 보는 사람들로부터 좀 떨어져 있고 싶었어.

get away from~ …을 멀리하다, 벗어나다

198
I just wish I had the guts to do it.
내가 그걸 할 배짱이 있었으면 좋겠어.

have the guts to~ …할 배짱이 있다

199
I kid you not, man.
농담아냐, 이 친구야.

200
I know how you feel. My mother makes me crazy. 그 심정 알겠어. 우리 엄마도 날 미치게 해.

I know how you feel (about~) 네가 (…에 대해) 어떤 기분인지 알아

201
I know I was wrong to get drunk at the party.
파티에서 술취하는 것은 잘못이라는 걸 알아.

get drunk 취하다 get tipsy 가볍게 취하다

202
I know I'm being a prat.
내가 멍청하게 굴었다는거 알아.

203

I know it is, but I've learned my lesson.
그건 알아, 하지만 난 교훈을 얻었어.

learn one's lesson 교훈을 얻다

204

I know it was a cheap shot, but I feel so much better now. 치사했던 건 알지만 기분은 훨씬 좋네.

be a cheap shot 비열하다, 치사하다

205

I know just how you feel.
어떤 심정인지 알겠어.

206

I know Mike like the back of my hand.
난 마이크를 속속들이 잘 알고 있지.

know sb[sth] like the back of one's hand 잘 알고 있다

207

I know that it weirds you out.
그 때문에 너 기분이 이상하다는거 알아.

weird sb out …을 정신나가게 하다, 불안하게 하다

208

I know that look. What's up?
나 그 표정 알아. 무슨 일이야?

What's up? 잘 지내?, 무슨 일이야?

209
I know that you have issues with your dad.
네가 아버지와 문제가 있는거 알고 있어.

I have issues with sb[sth] …와 문제가 있다

210
I know that's a hand-me-down ring.
그건 대대로 물려받는 반지인 걸 알아.

211
I know what I'm doing.
나도 아니까 걱정하지마, 내가 다 알아서 할게.

212
I know what I'm saying.
나도 알고 하는 말이야.

213
I know what you mean. My wife does the same thing. 무슨 말인지 알아. 아내도 그래.

I know what you mean 무슨 말인지 알겠어

214
I know what you're up to.
네 속셈 다 알아.

215

I know you can beat this baseball team, so go get 'em! 네가 이 야구팀을 이길 수 있다는 걸 알아, 그러니 힘내라!

Go get 'em! 힘내라 = Go get them!

216

I know you don't like dancing, but give it a whirl. 너 춤추는거 싫어하는거 알지만 한번 해봐.

give it a whirl 한번 해보다

217

I know you think that she was the one.

걔가 네 짝이었다고 생각한다는 걸 알아.

Sb be the one하게 되면 「…분이야」, 즉 자기가 찾던 「자기 짝이다」, 「이상형이다」라는 의미가 된다.

218

I know you've never been to college.

난 네가 대학에 다녀본 적이 없다는 것을 알고 있어.

219

I know, so that was kind of a bummer.

알아, 그럼 좀 실망스러운데.

be a bummer 실망스럽다

220

I know, the clock is ticking.

나도 알아, 시간이 없어.

221
I left my phone in my office.
핸드폰을 사무실에 두고 왔네.

222
I like many women. That's my thing.
난 많은 여자들을 좋아해. 내 전문이지.

That's my thing 내 전공이지, 내 전문이야

223
I like this part.
난 이런게 좋더라.

224
I look forward to waking up to a clean house tomorrow. 난 내일 일어나 깨끗한 집을 보게 되길 기대해.

look forward to~ …을 기대하다

225
I lost track of time.
몇시인지 놓쳤어.

lose track of time 몇시인지 시간을 놓치다

226
I love playing poker. I'm in.
나 포커치는거 좋아해. 나도 할게.

I'm in 나 할게 = Count me in

227

I love the way he used to boss around Alice.
걔가 앨리스한테 이래라 저래라 하던 방식이 좋아.

bossy 으시대는 boss around 이래라 저래라하다

228

I lowered the price. Will that do it?
내가 가격을 낮췄는데 그거면 충분하겠어?

Will that do (it)? 그거면 충분해?

229

I made a major decision.
난 아주 중요한 결정을 했어.

230

I made a reservation for a party of three at 9 pm. 저녁 9시에 3인석을 예약해놨는데요.

231

I made it!
(쉽지 않은 일을) 해냈어!

232

I made us a lot of money! Who's your daddy?
난 돈 많이 벌었어! 대단하지?

Who's your daddy? 나 대단하지?

233
I make no excuse for the choices I have made.
내가 한 선택에 대해 변명의 여지가 없어.

That's no excuse 변명이 안돼 (=That's not an excuse = make no excuse)

234
I mean it.
정말이야, 진심이야, 분명히 말했어.

235
I mean, technology's not my thing.
내 말은 기술은 내가 싫어하는거야.

That's not my thing 질색이야, 싫어해 = That's not my cup of tea

236
I mean, things are going well.
내 말은 상황이 잘 돌아가고 있다고.

go well 잘되다

237
I mean, we can get laid anytime we want.
내 말은 우린 원하면 언제라도 섹스를 할 수 있다는거야.

get laid 섹스하다 = get lucky, a good[easy] lay 좋은[쉬운] 잠자리 상대

238
I might get a job at Google.
나 구글에 취직할지도 몰라.

get a job at~ …에 취직하다

239

I must say, I never realized your job was so difficult. 네 일이 그렇게 힘든 줄 몰랐다고 해야 되겠네.

I must say, S+V …라고 해야 되겠어

240

I need sex now. You know what I mean?

지금 나 섹스해야 돼. 무슨 말인지 알지?

You know what I mean(?) 무슨 말인지 알지(?) if you know what I mean 내 말이 뭔지 안다면

241

I need to get ahead of the other competitors.

다른 경쟁자들을 앞질러야 해.

be[get] ahead of …보다 앞서다, 능가하다

242

I need to get some sleep.

난 잠을 좀 자야겠어.

get some sleep 잠을 좀 자다

243

I need you to get this right.

이거 제대로 처리해요.

get it right 일을 제대로 하다, 똑바로 일처리하다

244

I need your help! I'm in big trouble!

네 도움이 필요해! 큰 어려움에 빠졌어!

be[get] in big[real] trouble 큰 곤경에 처하다

245
I never heard of such a thing.
그런 얘긴 처음 들어봐. 말도 안돼.

246
I never realized how pathetic you are.
네가 얼마나 한심한지 난 전혀 몰랐어.

247
I normally don't do this, but I'm desperate.
보통 이러지 않지만 내가 절박해서.

do this 이렇게 하다

248
I once made out with a stranger in an elevator.
한번은 엘리베이터에서 모르는 사람과 애무한 적 있어.

make out with sb …와 애무하다

249
I owe you an apology. I don't know how I can make it up to you.
사과할게. 어떻게 보상해야 할지 모르겠어.

I owe you an apology 내가 사과할게 ⇔ You owe me an apology 넌 내게 사과해야 돼

250
I owe you nothing. Shut up. Get out of here.
네 덕본 거 하나도 없어. 입닥치고 꺼져.

Shut up (about~)! 닥쳐!

251
I pity you.
네가 불쌍해, 네가 안됐어.

252
I plan to ask my girlfriend to marry me.
난 여친에게 청혼할 계획이야.

ask sb to marry me …에게 결혼하자고 하다

253
I promise you! He said he was coming.
정말이야! 온다고 했어.

(I) Promise! 정말이야! 약속할게! = I promise you!

254
I pulled a fast one on her.
내가 걔한테 사기쳤어.

pull a fast one on sb …을 속이다, 사기치다, 등치다

255
I really appreciate this.
정말 고마워.

256
I really enjoyed your company.
함께 있어서 정말 즐거웠어요.

257
I really fancy her.
난 정말 걔를 좋아해.

fancy …을 좋아하다

258
I really suck at putting my emotions into words.
난 내 감정을 말로 나타내는 것에 정말 어눌해.

suck at~ …에 서투르다, 젬병이다

259
I saw you making out in the car.
네가 차에서 애무하는거 봤어.

make out은 유명숙어로 「이해하다」, 「…인 척하다」 등으로 잘 알려져 있으나, 스크린에서는 남녀간에 키스 및 touching, rubbing 등을 의미한다.

260
I scoped it out.
내가 자세히 들여다봤어.

scope out 자세히 검토하다

261
I screwed up. Chris, haven't you ever screwed up?
내가 일을 그르쳤어. 크리스, 넌 망친 적 없어?

screw up 망치다, 실수하다 be screwed up 엉망이 되다

262
I see where this is going.
무슨 말을 하려는지 알겠어.

where가 come이나 go 동사와 합쳐지면 의미가 비유적으로 변한 경우.

263
I see your point, I'm all right with it.
네 말뜻을 알겠어. 난 괜찮아.

Am I right?(내가 맞아?) vs. I'm all right(괜찮아 = That's okay)

264
I see your point. Wait, what's your point?
네 말을 알겠는데 요점이 뭐였지?

What's your point? 무슨 말을 하려는거야? What's the point? 요점이 뭐야?

265
I should just get on with ordinary life.
난 일상의 삶을 계속 살아가야 돼.

get on with sth …을 계속하다

266
I should probably take this.
이 전화 받아야 될 것 같아.

I got to get that 이 전화 받아야 돼 take[get] the call 전화를 받다

267
I should warn you. I'm not very good at this.
미리 말해두지만 나 이거 잘 못해.

be good[great, terrific] at~ …을 잘하다, 능하다

268
I shouldn't have run out on you.
난 널 그렇게 두고 달아나지 말았어야 했는데.

run out on sb 저버리고 달아나다

269
I shouldn't have said that.
그걸 말하지 말았어야 했는데.

shouldn't have+pp …하지 말았어야 했는데 하고 말았다

270
I sorta did a stupid thing last night.
내가 어젯밤에 좀 멍청한 짓을 저질렀어.

271
I spend Valentine's Day catching up on work and stuff.
발렌타인 데이에는 밀린 일 등을 하면서 보내.

catch up on 밀린 일을 하다

272
I split up with my girlfriend.
나 여자친구랑 헤어졌어.

split up with sb (…와 관계, 결혼 등을) 끝내다, 갈라서다

273
I stood in for Dwight while he was away.
난 드와이트가 자리를 비운 사이 걔 일을 대신 해줬어.

stand in for sb …대신 일을 봐주다

274

I suppose so. Especially after our last phone call. 그런 것 같아. 특히 우리가 지난번에 통화한 이후에.

I suppose so 그래도 돼요, 그런 것 같아

275

I suppose that doesn't matter to you, does it?

너한테 상관없잖아, 그지?

It doesn't matter to sb (wh~) …에게 (…는) 중요하지 않아, 상관없어

276

I swear to God, I am done with guys like that.

하늘에 두고 맹세하는데, 저런 놈들하고는 끝이야.

swear on sb[sth] …을 걸고 맹세하다 I swear on sb[sth] S+V …을 걸고 …을 맹세해

277

I take it back.

취소할게.

278

I tend to have a bit of an eye for these things.

난 이런 것들을 보는 눈이 좀 있는 편이야.

tend to …하는 경향이 있다, 보살피다(= care for)

279

I think I should go check it out.

내가 가서 한 번 점검해봐야 할 것 같아.

check it out 확인하다 Check it out! 이것 좀 봐!

280
I think I will pass.
난 사양할게. 난 됐어.

281
I think I'll go for "yes." Thank you for asking me. 예스로 할 것 같아. 물어봐줘서 고마워.

go for sth 선택하다(choose)

282
I think it's time for you to settle down.
네가 이제 자리 잡아야 할 때라고 생각해.

settle down 자리에 앉다, 진정하다, 정착하다

283
I think maybe it's better just to stop building it up and just say it. 난 그만 포장하고 그냥 말하는게 나을 것 같아.

build it up 인상적이게끔 포장해서 말하다

284
I think that I'm going to turn in right now, if you don't mind. 괜찮다면 난 지금 잠자리에 들고 싶어.

If you don't mind, 네가 괜찮다면,

285
I think that shirt isn't a good match for you. No offense. 그 셔츠가 너와 안 어울리는 것 같아. 기분 나빠하지마.

No offense 오해하지마, 기분나빠하지마

286

I think they're getting in the way of our friendship. 난 그것들이 우리 우정에 방해되는 것 같아.

get[be] in the way of~ …에 방해가 되다

287

I think we are so on the right track!

우린 아주 올바른 방향으로 가는 것 같아!

You're on the right track 잘하고 있어

288

I think we should just get it out of the way now. 이제 우리 빨리 해결해버리는게 나을 것 같아.

get it out of the way 해치우다, 털어놓다

289

I think we should stop seeing each other.

우리 그만 만나야 될 것 같아.

stop seeing sb 그만 만나다

290

I think what you're saying is bullshit.

네가 하는 말은 말도 안된다고 생각해.

(That's) Bullshit! 거짓말!, 허튼 소리하지마!

291

I think you've mistaken me for someone else.

저를 다른 사람과 착각하신 것 같네요.

mistake A for B A를 B로 착각하다

292
I thought I might ask if we could have another go. 우리가 다시 할 수 있을지 물어볼까 생각했어.

have another go 다시 하다

293
I thought it was like a vitamin or something.
난 그게 비타민이나 뭐 그런 것인 줄 알았어.

~, or something 뭐 그런거 , or something은 「…인지 무엇인지」, 「뭐 그런 거」 등이라는 의미. 비슷한 의미로는 "뭐 그런 류의 얘기였어"라는 뜻의 ~words to that effect가 있다. 이는 ~or something to that effect라 쓰기도 한다.

294
I toId him I'd seen better.
별로라고 걔한테 말했어.

I've seen better 이건 별로야, 그저 그래 I've seen worse 괜찮은 편이다

295
I told her to drop by for a drink.
난 걔보고 잠깐 들러 술 한잔하자고 했어.

come by 잠시 들르다 = stop by[in, off], drop by[in, around]

296
I told her you were otherwise engaged.
난 걔에게 네가 다른 일로 바쁘다고 했어.

be engaged 다른 일을 하고 있다

297

I told him to stay away from Cindy.
난 걔한테 신디로부터 떨어져 있으라고 했어.

stay away from~ …에 가까이 하지 않다, …에 얼씬거리지 않다

298

I took the liberty of declining it.
난 내 맘대로 그걸 취소했어.

take the liberty of~ 실례를 무릅쓰고 …하다, 제멋대로 …하다, 마음대로 …하다, 허락도 없이 …하다

299

I tried to tell her she was mistaken.
난 걔한테 걔가 잘못했다고 말하려고 했어.

I'm much mistaken 내가 잘못 생각했어

300

I try to take care of my family.
내 가족을 돌보려고 해.

take care of sb 돌보다. 범죄집단에서 take care of sb하게 되면 「…을 처리하다」, 「살해하다」라는 뜻이 된다.

301

I understood everything. I had it all sussed.
난 모든 걸 이해했어. 모든 것을 이해했다고.

suss 이해하다

302

I wanna soldier on in spite of the injury.
부상에도 불구하고 난 견디고 싶어.

I wanna soldier on 난 견디고 싶어

303
I want no part of it.
난 그 일에 관여하고 싶지 않아.

304
I want nothing else to do with you, Tom. It's over.
탐, 너랑 엮이고 싶지 않아. 끝이야.

헤어진 사람을 잊는다라고 할 때는 be over 혹은 get over라고 하면 된다.

305
I want to ask Chris out on a date.
크리스에게 데이트 신청하고 싶어.

ask sb out on a date …에게 데이트 신청하다

306
I want to get her back.
난 그녀를 되찾고 싶어.

get sb back 되찾다 get back to London 런던으로 돌아가다

307
I want to make it right.
난 그것을 제대로 바로잡고 싶어.

make it right 일을 제대로 바로 잡다

308
I want to move on. I don't want to go backwards.
다음으로 넘어가고 싶어. 뒤로 돌아가고 싶지 않아.

move on (to~) 잊다, 다음으로 넘어가다

309

I want to quit, but then I think I should stick it out. 그만두고 싶지만 계속 참고 견뎌야 될 듯해.

stick it out 참다, 버티다

310

I want to take you out for a drink tonight.
오늘밤 같이 한잔했으면 하는데.

invite[take] sb out for a drink 술마시자고 초대하다[데리고 나가다]

311

I want you to move in with me.
나랑 함께 살자.

move in (with) 이사해오다, 동거하다(move in together)

312

I wanted to clear that up with you.
난 너와 그 문제를 해결하고 싶었어.

clear sth up 문제를 해결하다, 설명하다

313

I wanted to scare the hell out of him.
간 떨어질 정도로 걔를 놀라게 해주고 싶었어.

You scared the hell out of me! 간 떨어질 뻔했다!

314

I was being drawn to you.
난 네게 끌렸어.

be drawn to sb[sth] …에 끌리다

315

I was in love with him, truth be known.
사실을 말하자면 난 그를 사랑하게 되었어.

(if) truth be known[told] 사실을 말하자면

316

I was just about to say that.
안 그래도 그 얘기하려고 했어.

317

I was late because I couldn't figure out what to wear.
뭘 입을지 몰라서 늦었어.

figure it out 알아내다, 이해하다 figure out what~ …을 알아내다

318

I was on call last night. I didn't get much sleep.
어젯밤 비상대기였어. 잠을 많이 못 잤다구.

be on call 비상대기이다

319

I was really rooting for them.
난 그들을 정말로 응원했어.

root for (곤경에 처한) 사람을 응원하다

320

I was seeing someone back in London.
난 런던에 있을 때 만나는 사람이 있었어.

be seeing sb …와 사귀다, 만나다

321
I was so into her I couldn't think of anything else. 걔한테 너무 빠져 있어서 다른 것은 생각할 수도 없었지.

be into sb ···에 푹 빠지다

322
I was so wrapped up in my own personal life?
내가 너무 사생활에만 몰두해 있었나?

be wrapped up in~ ···에 몰입하다, ···에 빠지다

323
I was somewhere else.
잠시 딴 생각했어, 다른 곳에 있었어.

324
I was stuck at home.
난 집에 콕 박혀 있었어.

be stuck at~ ···에 걸리다, 갇혀 있다

325
I was thinking we could take in a film after this. 우리는 이거 후에 영화를 같이 볼 수 있을거라 생각했어.

take in 같이 보다

326
I was too stoned to understand what was going on. 난 너무 취해서 무슨 일인지 이해하지 못했어.

be stoned 약에 취하다 look wasted 약에 취하다

327
I was tricked. I was told there would be free booze. 난 속았어. 공짜술이 있을거라 들었거든.

trick sb 속여먹다, 속여서 …하다

328
I wasn't going to bring it up before sex.
난 섹스 전에는 그 얘기를 꺼내지 않을려고 했었어.

bring up 화제로 …을 꺼내다

329
I wasn't suggesting you're a slag or anything.
난 네가 매춘부나 뭐 그런 여자라고 말하는게 아녔어.

330
I went to college with the bride.
난 신부와 동창예요.

went to college with sb …와 동창이다

331
I will get you a present as soon as I get some money. 돈이 생기는 대로 너한테 선물을 사줄게.

You got sb a present? …에게 선물을 준다고?

332
I will not have sex with you! Not again!
난 너랑 섹스하지 않을거야! 다시는!

Not again! 다시는 그러지 않을거야!

333
I will not take this lying down.
난 이걸 그냥 받아들일 수는 없어.

take sth lying down 감수하고 받아들이다

334
I will try my luck.
(되든 안되든) 한번 해봐야겠어.

335
I wish I could figure out a way to get Tom off my back.
톰을 떨쳐낼 수 있는 방법을 찾아냈으면 좋겠어.

get off sb's back …을 괴롭히지 않다 get A off sb's back A를 떨쳐버리다

336
I won't believe it until I see it.
내가 볼 때까지는 믿지 않을거야.

I won't believe it 믿지 않을거야 You won't believe it 믿지 못할거야

337
I won't hold it against you.
널 원망하진 않을거야.

hold sth against sb (과거에 받은 상처로) 잊지 않고 계속 싫어하다

338
I wondered where it came from. That explains it.
어디서 온건가 그랬어. 이제 알겠구만.

That explains it 그럼 설명이 되네, 아 그래서 이런 거구나, 이제 알겠네

339

I work as a businessman, but that's not all I do.
비즈니스맨으로 일하지만, 그 일만 하는게 아냐.

That's not all I do 그것만 하는게 아냐

340

I work for myself as a freelance writer.
프리랜서 작가로 혼자 일해.

work as …로 일하다

341

I worked my ass off.
뼈빠지게 일했어, 죽도록 열심히 일했어.

V+one's ass off (~ing) (…하느라) 죽도록 …하다

342

I would have to talk myself into trying again.
내가 맘잡고 다시 해봐야 될 것 같아.

talk oneself into~ 맘 잡고 …하다(스스로 설득해서 …하게 만들다라고 생각하면 된다.)

343

I would say don't wait up, but you'll be asleep by 11:00.
안자고 기다리지 말라고 하려 했지만 넌 11시면 잠들거야.

wait up 자지않고 기다리다

344

I would say that that makes a lot of sense.
그건 정말 그럴듯하다고 해야겠어.

make sense 말이 된다, 일리가 있다   ~that that~ 앞의 것은 접속사, 뒤의 것은 지시대명사로 주어이다.

345

I wouldn't be the rebound guy.
난 땜빵용 애인은 되지 않을거야.

be a good rebound for sb …에게 아주 좋은 땜방용 사람이다

346

I wouldn't care about you tumbling into some mess with a girl.
네가 한 여자와 지저분하게 얽인다 해도 난 상관안할거야.

be (in) a mess 엉망이다, 곤경에 빠지다 clean up the mess 청소하다, 치우다

347

I wouldn't do it, but that's your call.
나 같으면 안하겠지만 네가 결정할 문제야.

It's your call 네가 결정할 문제이다

348

I wouldn't do that if I were you.
내가 너라면 안 그럴 걸.

I wouldn't do that 나라면 그렇게 하지 않을텐데

349

I wouldn't say that.
나라면 그렇게 말하지 않을텐데.

350

I wouldn't miss the celebration for the world.
그 기념식에는 꼭 가도록 할게.

I wouldn't have missed it for the world. 꼭 그렇게 했었을거야.

351
I wouldn't if I were you.
내가 너라면 그렇게 하지 않겠어.

352
I wouldn't put it past her.
걔는 능히 그러고도 남을 사람이야.

I wouldn't put it past sb to+V (부정적인 행동을) …가 하고도 남는다, 충분히 …할 사람이다

353
I('ve) got to get moving.
가봐야겠어.

354
I'd better get a move on it.
빨리 서둘러야겠어.

get a move on 서두르다, 가다

355
I'd better get back with Naomi.
나오미하고 다시 사귀어야겠어.

get back with sb …와 다시 사귀다   get back together 다시합치다

356
I'd kill for this job.
이 일만 할 수 있다면 뭐든지 하겠어.

357
I'd like that. That sounds sweet.
그럼 좋지. 고마워.

I'd love[like] that 그럼 좋지

358
I'd like to go for a walk. Do you mind?
산책하고 싶은데, 괜찮겠어?

Do you mind? 그만 좀 할래?, 괜찮겠어?

359
I'd like to know what this is all about.
이게 무슨 일인지 알고 싶어.

What's it all about? 왜 그래?, 무슨 일이야?

360
I'd like to propose a toast to the newly married couple.
신혼부부에게 축배를 합시다.

I'd like to propose[make] a toast to~ (…을 위해) 축배를 듭시다 결혼식이나 파티 때 축배나 건배를 들자고 할 때는 toast를 쓴다.

361
I'd rather not.
그렇고 싶지 않아.

362
I'll have the chicken teriyaki, well done.
치킨데리야끼 먹을래, 잘 익혀서.

well done 잘 익힌

363
I'll admit I was a little curt that night.
그날밤 내가 좀 퉁명스러웠던 건 인정할게요.

364
I'll ask her out. Would that bother you?
걔한테 데이트 신청할건데, 그러면 안되겠어?

Would that bother you? 그럼 방해가 되겠어요?

365
I'll be right there.
곧 갈게, 지금 가.

366
I'll be there for you when you have hard times.
네가 어려울 때 내가 힘이 되어줄게.

be there for sb …을 위해 힘이 되어주다

367
I'll be there.
갈게.

368
I'll boil it down for you.
간단히 얘기할게, 요점만 얘기할게.

369

I'll call back later.
내가 나중에 다시 전화할게.

370

I'll do some digging, I'll find out what it is.
내가 좀 조사해보고 그게 뭔지 알아낼게.

do some digging 조사해보다, 뒤져보다

371

I'll do whatever it takes.
어떻게 해서라도 할게.

do whatever it takes to~ 어떻게 해서라도 …을 하다

372

I'll get an A if I cheat on the exam.
시험에서 커닝하면 A 맞을 수 있어.

cheat on (시험) 부정행위를 하다, 바람피다 cheat 속임수, 편법, 사기꾼

373

I'll get on Wikipedia and look it up.
위키피디아에 검색해서 그걸 찾아볼게.

look (sth) up 정보를 찾다

374

I'll get out of your hair.
널 방해하지 않고 그만 갈게.

get[be, keep] out of sb's hair 폐끼치지 않고 그만 가다, 괴롭히지 않다

375
I'll get right on it.
당장 그렇게 하겠습니다.

376
I'll get some thoughts to you.
내 생각을 말해줄게.

get some thoughts (to, on)~ 생각을 …에게 전하다[말해주다]

377
I'll get to it, don't nag me.
바로할게, 들볶지마.

get to it 바로 하다 Let's get to it 한번 해보자

378
I'll give it some thought.
내가 좀 생각을 해볼게.

give sth some thought …을 생각 좀 해보다(give some thought to)

379
I'll give you a ride.
태워다 줄게.

give sb a ride[life] …을 태워다주다 get a ride 차를 얻어타다

380
I'll go along with that.
난 찬성야, 동의해.

go along with~ …에 동의하다

381
I'll go on a date with you.
나 너랑 사귈거야.
go (out) on a date with sb 사귀다

382
I'll have a poke around tonight.
오늘밤 내가 한번 찾아볼게.
do research 조사하다 = have a poke around

383
I'll have it with a side of French fries.
프렌치 프라이와 함께 그걸로 주세요.
I'll have it 그걸로 주세요 What can I get for you? 뭘 갖다드릴까요?

384
I'll have my car back in no time.
내 차를 즉시 되찾아야겠어.
in no time 즉시

385
I'll just break it off with her this week.
이번 주에 그냥 걔와 헤어질거야.
break it off 헤어지다

386
I'll just have to learn to live with it.
난 견디는 법을 배워야 할거야.
live with that[it] 견디다

387
I'll keep my fingers crossed (for you)!
행운을 빌어줄게!

keep one's fingers crossed 행운을 빌어주다 = Fingers crossed

388
I'll keep that in mind.
명심할게.

keep sth in mind 가슴에 새겨두다, 명심하다

389
I'll look you up next time I'm in New York.
내가 담에 뉴욕가면 들를게.

look up sb 방문하다, 들르다

390
I'll make some calls.
몇군데 전화 좀 해볼게.

make some calls 몇 군데 전화를 해보다, 전화 몇 통 해보다

391
I'll make up for it tomorrow, okay? I promise.
내가 내일 그거 보상할게, 응? 약속해.

make up for~ 보충하다, 보상하다 = make it up to

392
I'll nip his chances with Olivia right in the bud.
난 올리비아와 걔가 엮일 가능성을 사전에 방지할거야.

nip ~ in the bud 미연에 방지하다

393

I'll put you through right away.
바로 바꿔드릴게요.

put[patch] sb through 전화를 바꿔주다

394

I'll see what I can do.
알아보죠, 어디 한번 알아볼게요, 어떻게든 해볼게.

395

I'll see you later. Have a good one!
나중에 봐. 좋은 하루 보내고!

Have a good one! 좋은 하루 보내요! = Have a good day!

396

I'll take my chances.
위험부담을 감수하겠어, 모험을 해보겠어.

take a chance (to~) (…하는) 위험 부담을 감수하다

397

I'll take you to dinner. My treat.
저녁 먹으러 가자. 내가 낼게.

take sb to~ …을 …로 데리고 나가다

398

I'll take you up on that.
네 제안을 받아들일게.

399
I'll tell him to call you back as soon as he's free.
시간이 나는대로 전화하라고 전할게요.

call sb …에게 전화를 하다 call sb back …에게 콜백(답신) 전화를 하다

400
I'll tell you what. How about I cook dinner at my place?
이럼 어때 우리 집에서 저녁 해먹자?

(I'll) Tell you what 이게 어때, 실은 이래

401
I'll try not to slip up.
실수하지 않도록 할게.

slip up 주로 작은 실수를 하다

402
I'll walk you through it.
그걸 어떻게 하는지 방법을 알려줄게.

walk ~ through …에게 단계별로 설명해주다

403
I'll work on cooking, you clean the house.
내가 요리할테니 당신은 집청소해.

work on sth[~ing] …일을 하고 있어

404
I'm a cheap drunk.
난 금방 취하는 사람이야.

405

I'm afraid I've got some bad news.
안 좋은 소식이 좀 있어.

have[get] some bad news 안좋은 소식이 있다

406

I'm afraid it's a done deal.
이미 결정이 난거잖아.

(That's a) Done deal 그러기로 한거야, 다 끝난 얘기야

407

I'm all mixed up.
너무 혼란스러워, 모든 게 복잡해졌어.

be mixed up 혼란스럽다(= be confused)

408

I'm all right with that.
난 괜찮아.

409

I'm all yours. What's up?
얼마든지. 무슨 일이야?

I'm all yours 네가 원한다면 언제든지

410

I'm always on the market.
난 언제나 혼자야.

be on the market 임자가 없다, 애인이 없다

411

I'm an idiot? Says who?
내가 바보라고? 누가 그래?

Says who? 누가 그래? Says you! 바로 네 얘기야! Say what? 뭐라고?

412

I'm ashamed of you.
부끄러운 일이야. 부끄러워 혼났어. 너 때문에 너무 창피해.

413

I'm begging you, please leave my wife out of it. 제발 부탁해, 제발 내 아내를 그 일에서 빼줘.

I'm begging you 제발 부탁이야 I beg of you 제발

414

I'm bored out of my gourd!
지루해 죽겠어!

be bored out of one's gourd 지루해 죽겠다

415

I'm bored out of my mind.
지겨워 죽겠어.

be bored out of one's mind 지겨워[지루해] 죽겠다

416

I'm bringing a date, so I'll be off the market.
애인 데려오니까 난 품절남이야.

be off the market 임자가 있다

417
I'm clueless about Vicky's taste in sex.
난 비키의 성적 취향에 대해 아는게 없어.

be clueless about~ 전혀 몰라

418
I'm coming. I'm coming. Just hang on.
가, 간다고. 좀 만 기다려.

Hang on (a minute) 잠깐만. 전화상이나 일반상황에서 쓰이는 표현. 지금 내가 뭔가 다른 것을 하고 있으니 「잠시만 기다려 달라」고 하는 말이다.

419
I'm coming. What is it?
가, 뭔데?

I'm coming은 상대방에게 바로 가겠다는 기초표현

420
I'm cool with[about] that.
난 괜찮아, 상관없어.

421
I'm done with my choices.
선택을 했어.

I'm done (with) (…을) 끝냈어 I'm almost done 거의 끝냈어

422
I'm done with this.
이거 다 끝냈어, 그만하겠어, 이제 안해.

423

I'm done with you, Mike. Don't bother coming home.
난 너랑 끝났어, 마이크. 굳이 집에 올 필요 없어.

Don't bother to~[~ing] 굳이 …할 필요없어

424

I'm easy. Any French wine will be good.
난 상관없어. 프랑스 와인이라면 어떤 것도 좋아.

I'm easy 난 아무래도 좋아

425

I'm flattered, but I'm seeing somebody.
그렇게 말해줘서 고마운데, 나 지금 만나는 사람있어.

I'm flattered 그렇게 말해줘서 고마워요, 그렇지도 않아요

426

I'm fucking with you.
너한테 장난친거야.

fuck with sb 골리다, 장난치다

427

I'm getting back on my feet.
난 다시 일어나고 있어, 재기하고 있어.

get[be] back on one's feet 다시 일어서다, 재기하다

428

I'm getting back to the life I was supposed to have by now.
지금쯤 내가 살고 있어야 할 삶으로 돌아가는거야.

get back to the life~ …한 삶으로 돌아가다

429
I'm glad you feel that way.
그렇게 생각한다니 기뻐.

feel that way 그렇게 생각하다

430
I'm glad you guys were bonding.
너희들이 잘 지내고 있어 기뻐.

be bonding 유대관계가 좋다

431
I'm glad you talked me into this.
날 설득해서 이걸 하게 해줘서 고마워.

talk sb into~ …을 설득하여 …하도록 하게 하다

432
I'm glad you were able to get away today.
네가 오늘 쉴 수 있어 다행이야.

get away 벗어나 쉬다, 휴식을 취하다

433
I'm glad you're bonding with your grandparents. 네가 조부모님들과 좋게 지내서 기뻐.

be bonding with sb …와 잘 지내다

434
I'm going to bitch about the neighbor's loud music. 이웃집의 시끄러운 음악소리에 항의할거야.

bitch about[at] 불평하다 harp on 짜증나게 불평하다

435
I'm going to get some air.
바람 좀 쐴거야.

get some air 바람을 쐬다

436
I'm going to go back to where I came from.
내가 왔던 곳으로 난 돌아갈거야.

be back to~ …로 돌아가다

437
I'm going to hang out. I got it all planned out.
난 놀거야. 다 계획 잡아놨어.

hang out 놀다, 시간을 보내다

438
I'm going to have a baby.
난 애를 낳을거야.

have a baby 임신하다, 임신중이다(get up the duff)　be expecting 임신중이다

439
I'm going to have to blow you out too.
너와 절연해야 될 것 같아.

blow sb out 물리치다, 절연하다

440
I'm going to have to get this off my chest.
이거 털어놓고 말해야겠어.

get sth off one's chest 마음 속에 있는 것을 털어놓다

441
I'm going to lose my mind if I have to continue doing this.
이 일을 계속 해야 한다면 난 미쳐버릴거야.

lose one's mind 이성을 잃다

442
I'm going to tell you again, don't push it.
다시 말하는데, 밀어붙이지마.

Don't push it! 재촉하지마! push oneself too hard 무리하다

443
I'm going with it.
난 그것으로 하겠다.

444
I'm going. You will never see me again.
나 간다. 다시 못볼거야.

I'm going 나 간다, 나 갈거야[참석할거야] ↔ I'm not going

445
I'm gonna be starting a career from scratch.
난 밑바닥에서부터 경력을 쌓기 시작하게 될거야.

from scratch 맨손으로, 처음부터

446
I'm gonna get you for that.
네게 그거 되갚아줄거야.

get sb 이해하다, 연락이 닿다, 해코지하다

447

I'm gonna go down there and teach that guy a lesson. 내가 가서 저 자식에게 한수 단단히 가르쳐주겠어.

teach sb a lesson …에게 단단히 이르다, 하면 안된다는 것을 똑똑히 가르쳐주다

448

I'm gonna hold you to that.

그 약속 꼭 지켜야 돼.

hold sb to sth …가 …의 약속을 지키게 하다

449

I'm gonna stick around here for a while.

난 한동안 여기서 머무를거야.

stick around 머무르다

450

I'm gonna try to take that as a compliment.

난 그걸 칭찬으로 받아들이려고 할거야.

take that as a compliment 칭찬으로 알다

451

I'm grateful not to work at that company.

저 회사에서 일하지 않게 돼 감사해.

work at[in]~ …에서 일하다

452

I'm happy for you.

네가 잘돼서 나도 기뻐.

453
I'm having a little chat with her.
개랑 잠깐 이야기하는 중이야.

454
I'm here to help. What can I do for you?
내가 도와주러 왔는데. 뭘 도와줄까?

What can I do for you? 뭘 도와줄까?

455
I'm here to listen. Fire away.
여기 듣고 있으니 질문들 해봐.

fire away 질문을 퍼붓다

456
I'm in if you're in.
네가 들어오면 나도 낄게.

You're in 너도 하는거야

457
I'm in on it.
난 알고 있어. 난 관련되어 있어.

458
I'm in your head.
네 생각이 뭔지 다 알아.

be in one's head …의 생각이 뭔지 다 알다

459
I'm just a little behind. I can catch up, no sweat. 난 좀 뒤쳐졌는데 따라잡을 수 있어. 문제없어.

No sweat 문제없어, 걱정마

460
I'm just flipping out a little bit.
난 조금 화가 났을 뿐이야.

flip out 벌컥 화내다, 열광하다   get (oneself) worked up 화내다

461
I'm just kidding. This is great.
농담야. 이거 대단해.

I'm just kidding 농담이야

462
I'm just saying you never know what could happen. 내 말은 무슨 일이 일어날지 모른다는 말이야.

I'm just saying (that) S+V 내 말은 단지 …라는거야

463
I'm just saying that to be nice.
그건 그냥 선의로 말한거야.

464
I'm kind of tuckered out.
좀 많이 지쳤어.

be tuckered out 지칠대로 지치다, 뻗다

465
I'm listening. Talk fast.
듣고 있어. 빨리 말해.

I'm listening 어서 말해 I'm not listening 네 말 안들을래

466
I'm losing my mind.
내가 제 정신이 아냐.

467
I'm messing with you. You're such a baby.
내가 장난친거야. 넌 정말 애같아.

mess with 화나게 하다, 괴롭히다

468
I'm not allowed to do that.
난 그거 하면 안돼.

469
I'm not feeling well and I need to rest.
기분이 별로 좋지 않아서 쉬어야 되겠어.

be not well 몸이 안좋다 be not feeling well 기분이 안좋아

470
I'm not following what you said.
네가 무슨 말을 했는지 모르겠어.

I'm not following 무슨 말인지 모르겠어

471
I'm not going anywhere, sweetheart.
나 아무데도 안 가, 자기야.

472
I'm not going to let you ruin my family!
네가 내 가족을 망치게 놔두지 않을거야!

ruin one's family 가족을 망치다

473
I'm not good when it comes to breaking up with girls. 난 여친들과 헤어지는거에는 아주 서툴러.

when it comes to~ …에 관한 한

474
I'm not here to get you in trouble.
널 곤란하게 하려고 여기 온게 아냐.

get sb in trouble …을 곤경에 빠트리다

475
I'm not just big on Chinese food.
난 중국 음식을 그다지 좋아하지 않아.

be big on~ …을 아주 좋아하다

476
I'm not kidding. Those are their real names.
정말야. 그게 걔네 본명야.

I'm not kidding (you) 농담아냐, 정말야 = I'm kidding you not

477
I'm not like you.
난 너랑 달라.

478
I'm not sure we can get through this difficult time. 우리가 이 어려운 시기를 헤쳐나갈 수 있을지 모르겠어.

get through~ (…을) 이겨내다, 해내다, 끝내다

479
I'm not sure what you mean.
무슨 말인지 모르겠어.

480
I'm not taking this lying down.
난 이걸 참지 않을거야.

take sth lying down …을 감수하다, 참다, 가만히 있다

481
I'm off in 10 minutes.
나 10분 후에 간다.

be off 출발하다, 떠나다, 가다

482
I'm off the booze.
나 술 끊었어.

483

I'm off to make my mark on the world.
난 나가서 세상에 이름을 떨칠거야.

make one's mark 이름을 떨치다, 성공하다

484

I'm off to work in the morning.
아침에 일하러 나가.

be off to+V …하기 위해 가다, 출발하다

485

I'm on it.
내가 할게, 내가 처리 중이야.

486

I'm on my mobile, if you need me.
내가 필요하면 핸폰으로 연락해.

I'm on my mobile 핸폰으로 연락해

487

I'm on my way back now.
지금 돌아가는 중이야.

be on my way back~ …로 돌아가다

488

I'm out of here. Wish me luck.
나 갈게. 행운을 빌어줘.

Wish me luck! 행운을 빌어줘! Good luck! 행운이 있기를!

489

I'm pissed off.
열받아, 진절머리나.

490

I'm really looking forward to this.
정말 무척 기대하고 있어.

be looking forward to+명사[~ing] 몹시 …하기를 고대하다

491

I'm really not in the mood to see a movie anymore. **더 이상 영화를 볼 기분이 아냐.**

I'm not in the mood for[to do]~ …할 기분 아냐

492

I'm really sorry you had to join the club.
같은 처지가 돼서 정말 안됐어.

Join the club 나도 같은 처지야

493

I'm really ticked off.
정말 열받았어, 화났어.

be ticked off at …에게 화나다

494

I'm running out of time. I need to finish this.
시간이 부족해. 이걸 끝마쳐야 돼.

Time's up 시간 다 됐어 be[run] out of time 시간이 부족하다

495
I'm saying you know nothing about me.
내 말은 넌 나에 대해서 아무것도 모른다는 말이지.

What am I saying? 내가 무슨 말을 하는거지? I'm not saying that 내 말은 그게 아냐

496
I'm sick of this.
진절머리가 나.

497
I'm so into you.
나, 너한테 푹 빠져 있어.

be into …에 빠지다, 심취하다

498
I'm so mad about you.
난 너를 열렬히 좋아해.

be[get] mad 화내다, 사족을 못쓰다

499
I'm so out of it today!
난 오늘 도통 정신이 없어!

be out of it 졸리거나 피곤해서 정신이 없다

500
I'm so relieved to hear you say that.
네가 그렇게 말하는 걸 들으니 맘이 놓여.

I'm relieved (to+V) (…해서) 다행이야

501
I'm so sorry for your loss.
상심에 위로 드립니다.

502
I'm so sorry for what I said earlier.
아까 내가 한 말 정말 미안해.

503
I'm sorry but, that's really not my problem.
미안하지만 그건 내 문제가 아니야.

It's not my problem 그거 내 문제가 아냐, 상관없어 It's not a problem 문제도 아냐

504
I'm sorry for my profanity.
욕설을 해서 미안해.

profanity 불경한 말, 욕설

505
I'm sorry it didn't go well today.
미안하지만 오늘 그거 잘 안됐어.

506
I'm sorry to hear that.
안됐네, 유감이야.

507
I'm sorry, I don't get your logic.
미안하지만, 무슨 말인지 모르겠어.

Get your logic 무슨 말인지 알겠어

508
I'm sorry. I put you on the spot.
미안, 널 난처하게 만들었네.

put sb on the spot 곤혹스럽게 하다

509
I'm sorry. I've just been so busy with work.
미안해. 난 일하느라 너무 바빴어.

be busy with[~ing] …하느라 바쁘다

510
I'm sorry? What did you say?
뭐라고? 뭐라고 했어?

What did you say? 뭐라고?

511
I'm stalking the wrong woman. I am such a dingus! 엉뚱한 여자를 스토킹했네. 이런 얼간이 같으니라구!

dingus 멍청이, 얼간이

512
I'm standing behind you.
네게 힘이 되어줄게.

stand behind sb …을 지원하다, 지지하다

513
I'm stuffed.
배가 불러.

514
I'm supposed to pick up a couple things.
몇가지 가지고 가야 돼요.
I am supposed to+V …해야 한다

515
I'm sure as shit happy to be home.
난 분명히 집에 오게 돼서 기뻐.
sure as shit 분명히

516
I'm sure that Dad is pissed.
아버지가 화나셨겠죠.
be[get] pissed (off, at) (…에) 화나다

517
I'm surprised to see you. To what do I owe this pleasure? **널보고 깜짝 놀랐네. 어인 행차신가?**
좀 구식이긴 하지만 가끔 나오는 To what do I owe this pleasure?는 방문하는 사람에게 정중하게 혹은 문맥에 따라 비아냥거리는 의미.

518
I'm not into guys.
난 남자애들에게 관심없어.
be not into~ …에 관심없다

519
I'm talking to you!
내 말 안들려!, 너한테 말하는 거야!, 내가 하는 말 좀 잘 들어봐!

520
I'm telling you, something's wrong!
잘 들어, 뭔가 이상해!
I'm telling you, 정말이야, 잘 들어 I'm telling you S+V 정말이지 …야

521
I'm through with taking your advice.
네 조언은 이제 안 받는다.
be through (with~) (…을) 끝내다, 끝나다

522
I'm trying to make a good impression.
좋은 인상을 주려고 노력하고 있어.
make a good[bad] impression 좋은[나쁜] 인상을 주다

523
I'm very busy. Is that all?
나 바빠. 그게 다야?
Is that all? 그게 다야?

524
I'm very sorry. I did not mean any harm.
미안. 피해를 줄려는 건 아니었어.
I didn't mean any harm 피해를 줄 생각은 없었어

525

I'm well aware of that. But there's nothing I can do. 난 잘 알고 있어. 하지만 내가 할 수 있는게 아무것도 없어.

I'm aware of it[that] …을 알고 있어

526

I'm well shot of the problems I had last years.
난 과거에 있었던 문제들을 다 잊어버렸어.

be well shot of sb …을 잊어버리다

527

I'm working on it.
지금 하고 있어.

work on ~ …일을 하다, 담당하다, 맡다

528

I've been dealing with that real estate thing.
전 부동산 관련 일들을 처리해왔습니다.

529

I've been meaning to call you.
그렇지 않아도 전화하려고 했는데.

530

I've been so gloomy since I broke up with my boyfriend. 내 남친과 헤어진 이후에 너무 우울해.

get gloomy 우울하다 be down in the mouth 의기소침하다

531

I've been there. You need to look for something better. 그 심정 이해해. 더 좋은 걸 찾아봐.

I've been there 1. 나도 그런 적 있어, 정말 그 심정 이해해 2. 가본 적 있어

532

I've been thinking about you all day.
난 종일 너만 생각했어.

I've been thinking about~ …을 생각 중이었어

533

I've been thinking, and come to some conclusions. 난 생각을 했고 어떤 결론에 다다랐어.

I've been thinking 생각 중이었어

534

I've been winging it with you for 18 years.
난 18년동안 너와 대충 살아왔어.

wing it 준비없이 대충하다, 그때그때 맞춰 살다

535

I've come this close to winning.
난 거의 승리 할 뻔했어.

be[come] this close to~ 거의 …할 뻔하다, …할 지경이다

536

I've done my fair share.
난 내 몫을 했어.

do one's fair share …의 몫을 하다

537

I've got a bone to pick with you.
너한테 불만 있어.

get a bone to pick with sb …에게 따질 일이 있다, 불만이 있다

538

I've got a crush on you.
난 너한테 반했어.

have[get] a crush on sb …에게 푹 빠지다

539

I've got a feeling she will not show up.
걔가 오지 않을 것 같은 느낌이 들어.

show up은 모임이나 회의 혹은 약속장소에 약속대로 「나타나다」, 「오다」라는 의미. 같은 표현으로는 turn up이 있다.

540

I've got an appointment with Brad at lunch time. 브래드와 점심 때 약속있어.

have an appointment with ~ …와 약속[예약]이 되어 있다

541

I've got an important announcement to make.
중요한 발표가 있어.

have~ to make 해야 할 …가 있어

542

I've got news for you.
새로운 소식있어, 놀랄만한 소식이 있어.

543
I've got to hand it to you!
너 정말 대단하구나!, 나 너한테 두 손 들었어!

544
I've got to pack.
난 짐을 싸야 돼.

pack 짐을 싸다

545
I've got your back, okay? You're not alone.
너 뒤를 봐줄게. 넌 혼자가 아냐.

I got your back 네 뒤를 봐줄게

546
I've gotta run. See you tomorrow.
나 가야 돼. 내일 봐.

I've gotta run 나 빨리 가야 돼

547
I've had enough of you. Leave me alone.
너한테 질린다. 좀 가만히 놔둬.

Leave me alone! 나 좀 내버려둬!

548
I've just seen the girl who broke my heart five years ago. 5년 전에 내 맘을 아프게 한 여자를 방금 봤어.

break one's heart 가슴을 아프게 하다

549
I've never seen anything like it[this, that].
그런 건 처음 봐.

550
I've paid my dues.
내 할 몫(책임)은 다했어, 값을 치렀어.

pay one's dues 빚을 갚다, 값을 치루다

551
I've sort of had feelings for you.
너한테 조금이지만 감정이 생겼어.

sort of 약간, 조금 = kind of

552
I've still got it.
나 아직 여전해.

553
I've tried and tried, but I can't come up with a solution.
계속 해봤는데, 답이 안 나와.

come up with sth은 유명한 숙어로 「좋은 아이디어나 계획을 생각해내는 것」을 말한다.

554
If anything happens.
무슨 일이 생기면.

555
If I promise to behave, can we still hang out?
내가 조신하게 행동한다고 약속하면 우리 같이 다니는거지?

I promise S+V 정말이지 …야, …을 약속할게 promise to+V …을 약속하다

556
If I were you, I would put my career before men. 내가 너라면 남자보다 일을 중요시하겠어.

put A before B B보다 A를 중요시하다

557
If it helps, I can loan you money until you get paid. 그렇게 해서 도움이 된다면 내가 너한테 돈을 빌려줄 수 있어.

if it helps 그게 도움이 된다면, 그렇게 해서 네가 편해진다면 get paid 돈을 받다

558
If it's not too much trouble.
수고스럽지 않다면.

559
If it's okay with you, I'd like to tag along.
괜찮다면 따라가고 싶어.

tag long 따라가다

560
If Jack doesn't stop eating all of the time, he'll turn into a fat person.
잭이 시도 때도 없이 먹는 걸 그만두지 않는다면 뚱보가 될거야.

turn into …이 되다

561

If someone's meant to be yours, eventually they will be. 누군가 너의 짝이라면 결국 그렇게 될거야.

be meant to be (together) 천생연분 = be made for each other

562

If there's any part of you that isn't sure, even now, say the word.

맘 한 구석에 확실하지 않은 부분이 있다면 지금이라도 그냥 말해.

Just say the word 말만해

563

If we're very careful, it shouldn't do any harm.

우리가 주의를 많이 기울이면, 아무런 해를 끼치지 않을거야.

do harm 해를 끼치다

564

If worse comes to worst.

최악의 경우에는, 아무리 어려워도.

565

If you ask me, I think he complains too much.

내 생각은 걔가 불평을 너무 많이 하는 것 같아.

If you ask me 내 생각에는   the way I see it 내가 보기에는

566

If you blow up, you'll blow it.

화를 내면 일을 망칠 걸.

blow it 기회 등을 날리다, 망치다   blow up 화내다   blow sb off 바람맞히다

567

If you don't mind my asking, when did you and John meet? 이런 말해서 그렇지만, 언제 존을 만났나요?

If you don't mind me[my] asking[saying] 내가 물어봐도 괜찮다면

568

If you don't mind, I'd like to ask you both a few questions. 괜찮다면 너희 둘에게 질문 좀 할게.

If you don't mind, I'd like to~ 네가 괜찮다면 …하고 싶어

569

If you know anything, I am begging you to tell me. 뭐 좀 아는게 있으면 제발이지 내게 말해줘.

I'm begging you to+V 제발 부탁인데 …해줘

570

If you want it, it's all yours.
그걸 원한다면, 너 가져.

It's all yours 그건 네 책임이야, 그건 네꺼야

571

If you want to see me, all you have to do is ask. 나 보고 싶으면 말만 하면 돼.

All you have to do is ask 말만 하면 돼

572

If you want to stay here, then shut your mouth! 여기 머무르고 싶으면 입닥치고 있어!

Shut your mouth[face]! 입닥쳐!

573

If you were in my position, what would you do? 내 처지라면 넌 어떻게 하겠어?

If you were in my position, 내 입장이라면,

574

If you're ready to talk, hit me with it.
말할 준비가 됐으면 어서 말해봐.

Hit me with it 어서 말해봐

575

If your mind doesn't grow old, people never grow old. 마음이 늙지 않으면 사람은 영원히 늙지 않을거야.

576

Is it crazy to think like that?
그렇게 생각하다니 미친걸까?

be crazy to+V …하다니 미쳤다, 제정신이 아니다

577

Is it okay with you if I set him up on a date?
걔 미팅시켜줘도 너 괜찮겠어?

set sb up …을 소개시켜주다 set sb up on a date 소개시켜주다

578

Is something wrong?
뭔가 잘못됐어?

be wrong 잘못되거나 틀리다

579
Is that [it] too much to ask?
내가 너무 많이 요구하는거야?

580
Is that something you're making up?
이게 네가 꾸미고 있는거야?

make up 화장하다, 얘기를 지어내다, 꾸며내다, 화해하다

581
Is that what I think it is?
내가 생각하는 그거 맞지?, 이게 정말 맞아?

582
Is that what you're saying?
네가 말하는게 이 말이야?

583
Is that why you don't want to get involved with me?
그래서 나와 사귀지 않으려고 한거야?

get[be] involved with sb~ …와 연인 사이다

584
Is this some kind of joke?
장난하는거지?, 나 놀리는거지?

585

It (completely) slipped my mind.
깜박 잊었어.

Sth slips one's mind …가 …을 깜박 잊다

586

It all adds up.
계산이 맞다, 앞뒤가 들어 맞아.

587

It blows my mind!
정신을 못차리겠어!, 마음이 설레네!

blow one's mind 흥분하거나 당황하여 어쩔 줄 모르다, 놀래키다

588

It could happen.
그럴 수도 있겠지, 그런 일이 있을 수도 있지.

589

It couldn't be better. I love it.
최고야. 정말 좋아.

Never been better 최상이다(= Never better = Couldn't be better)
can't get any worse 더 이상 나빠질 수 없다

590

It doesn't matter. That's not the point.
그건 상관없어. 그게 중요한게 아니잖아.

That's the point 그게 요점이야 That's not the point 요점은 그게 아냐

591
It doesn't matter. You decide.
상관없어. 네가 결정해.
It doesn't matter 중요하지 않아, 상관없어

592
It got me thinking about my own relationships.
그 때문에 내가 했던 연애들이 생각이 났어.
It got sb thinking of[about] ~ing …가 …을 생각하게 하다, …할 생각이 들어

593
It happens.
그러는거지, 그럴 수도 있지 뭐.

594
It is such a relief to finally know everything.
마침내 모든 걸 알게 되어 정말 안심야.
That[It]'s a relief (to+V) (…해서) 다행이야

595
It is written all over your face.
네 얼굴에 다 써있어.

596
It isn't worth the trouble.
괜히 번거롭기만 할거야.

597
It just kept getting worse and worse.
그냥 상황이 더 악화되고 있어.

be getting worse 점점 나빠지다

598
It just seems that you two belong together.
너희 둘 연인사이인 것 같아.

belong together 연인사이이다

599
It kinda grows on you.
넌 그걸 점점 좋아하는구나.

600
It might not be possible. Let me think about it.
가능하지 않을 수도 있어. 내가 생각해볼게.

Let me think about it 내가 생각해볼게 = I'll think about it

601
It never crossed my mind that he was lying.
걔가 거짓말하고 있다는 생각은 해보지도 못했어.

It never crossed my mind that S+V …은 생각도 못했어

602
It really is only going to take a minute.
정말이지 금방이면 될거야.

This[It] will just take a second 잠깐이면 돼

603
It really meant a lot to her.
그건 걔한테 정말 중요했어.

mean much to sb …에게 소중[중요]하다

604
It serves you right!
넌 그런 일 당해도 싸!, 꼴 좋다!, 샘통이다!

605
It suits me (fine).
난 좋아.

606
It took me months to make it with her.
걔와 자는데 몇달 걸렸어.

make it with sb …와 섹스하다

607
It took you all night to come up with that plan?
그 계획을 짜내는 데 하룻밤 꼬박 걸렸다구?

come up with 고안해내다, 따라잡다

608
It was a long shot.
승산이 희박했어, 가능성이 없었어.

609

It was a matter of time before she was promoted. 걘 승진하는 것은 시간문제였어.

get[be] promoted 승진하다

610

It was a slip of the tongue.
실언했어, 말이 잘못 나왔네.

611

It was fun having you.
같이 해서 즐거웠어.

This is[was] funny 재미있(었)어 That's not funny 우스워, 이상해

612

It was my mistake.
내 잘못이야.

613

It was the last thing I expected.
생각도 못했어.

614

It will take a lot of courage to do that.
그거 하려면 많은 용기가 필요할거야.

take (a lot of) courage to+V 용기를 내서 …하다

615

It won't take long.
오래 안 걸려.

616

It works for me.
내겐 효과적이야.

sth works for sb 효과적이다, 먹히다, 도움이 되다

617

It would really mean a lot to me if you guys came. 너희들이 오면 정말 큰 의미가 될거야.

I'd really mean a lot to me if you~ 네가 …한다면 정말 고맙겠어

618

It'll be a very big deal to me. Please. Stay.
이건 나한테 아주 중요한 일이야. 제발 남아줘.

big deal 중요한 일   a huge deal 거물

619

It'll be difficult, but I'll do what I can.
어렵겠지만 내가 어떻게 해볼게.

I'll do what I can 내가 해볼게

620

It's a big problem. You know what I'm saying?
그건 큰 문제야. 무슨 말인지 알겠어?

You know what I'm saying? 무슨 말인지 알겠어? = See what I mean?

621
It's a hold up, so everybody keep still.
강도다, 다들 꼼짝마.

hold up 총으로 강도질하다(holdup 노상강도)

622
It's a trick, I know he's bluffing.
그건 사기야, 걔가 뻥치는거 알고 있어.

Is this a trick? 이거 속임수야? It's a trick 이거 사기야

623
It's a very hard one to call.
그건 정말이지 판단하기 어려운 일이야.

be hard to call 판단하기 어렵다

624
It's all been a bit of a whirlwind, hasn't it?
정신없이 일들이 이어졌어, 그렇지 않았어?

be a whirlwind 정신없이 많은 일들이 일어나다

625
It's all for the best.
앞으로 나아질거야.

be (all) for the best 그게 최선의 길이다, 잘하는 일이야

626
It's all or nothing.
이판사판야, 모 아니면 도야.

627
It's an easy answer. A no-brainer.
그건 답이 쉽지. 쉬운 결정야.
no-brainer 쉬운 결정

628
It's difficult, but this is your job.
어렵지만 이건 네가 할 일이야.
This[It] is your job 이건 네가 할 일이야 It's one hell of a job 힘든 일이야

629
It's done. Let's go.
끝난 일이야. 가자.
It's done 끝났어, 그렇게 할게, 다 됐어 = That's done

630
It's every man for himself.
(누가 도와주지 않으니) 각자 알아서 해야지.

631
It's for your own good. You'll thank me for it someday.
그건 너 자신을 위한거야. 언젠가 내게 고마워할거야.
be for one's good …을 위한 것이다

632
It's going out of business? How do you know that?
폐업한다고? 넌 어떻게 안거야?
How do you know that? 어떻게 안거야?

633
It's good to know that your parents are healthy. 네 부모님이 건강하다는걸 알게 돼 좋아.

(It's) Good to know that[wh~] …을 알게 돼서 기뻐, 다행이야

634
It's just a phase.
그냥 한때 저러는거야.

635
It's just one of those things.
흔한 일야, 어쩔 수 없는 일야, 있는 일들 중 하나야.

636
It's late. Where do you think you're going to?
늦었어. 도대체 어딜 가는거야?

Where do you think you're going (to)? (도대체) 어딜 가는거야?

637
It's like that.
그 경우와 비슷해, 그런 셈이야, 그런거야.

638
It's my bad. I should have called her last night.
내 잘못이야. 내가 지난밤 걔한테 전화했어야 했는데.

(That's) My bad 내가 잘못했어 It's my fault 내 실수야

639
It's my life. I call the shots.
내 인생이니 내가 결정할게.

call the shots 결정하다 be one's shot …가 결정할 일이다

640
It's never gonna work. They are too different.
잘 되지 않을거야. 너무나 서로 다른걸.

It's never gonna work 그렇게 되지 않을거야

641
It's nice of you to think of me like that.
나를 그렇게 생각해줘서 정말 고마워.

That's (very) nice[kind] of you 친절도 해라(How kind of you)

642
It's no big deal, I do it all the time.
별 일 아냐, 난 항상 그러는데.

do it all the time 항상 이래

643
It's none of your business!
상관 말라구!

644
It's normal to get cold feet before your wedding. 결혼식을 앞두고 긴장하는 것은 정상이야.

get cold feet 긴장하다

645
It's not about that.
그런 문제가 아냐, 요점은 그게 아니야.

646
It's not all it's cracked up to be.
사람들의 말처럼 그런 건 아니야.

not be all it's cracked up to be 소문만큼 좋지 않다, 기대에 못미치다

647
It's not easy to get ahead at your job.
직장에서 성공하는 것은 쉽지 않아.

get ahead 성공하다

648
It's not gonna happen. Not in a million years.
절대 그럴 일 없을거야. 절대로.

(It's) Not gonna happen 그럴 일 없을거야

649
It's not gonna make any difference.
전혀 상관없어, 그래봤자 달라질 것 없어.

650
It's not good to hear the manager calling people names. 매니저가 사람들 욕하는 것을 듣는 것은 좋지 않아.

call sb names 욕하다, 험담하다 call one's name …의 이름을 부르다

651
It's not in the cards for me.
내게 그렇게 준비되어 있지 않아.

be in the cards 예상했던 일이다, 있을 수 있는 일이다

652
It's not like that. We're together.
그런게 아냐. 우리 같이 있어.

It's not like that 그런게 아냐

653
It's not my place.
내가 상관할 바가 아니다, 내가 나설 자리가 아냐.

654
It's not okay. You just caught me off guard.
괜찮지 않아. 전혀 예상치 못한 일이야.

catch sb off guard 전혀 예상하지 못한 일이다

655
It's not quite that she is foolish.
걔는 전혀 멍청하지가 않아.

Not quite that 전혀 그렇지 않아

656
It's not that bad after all.
그건 전혀 나쁘지 않았어.

Not bad 괜찮은데, 나쁘지 않아

657
It's not that simple.
그렇게 단순하지 않아.
It's not that 그런게 아냐　It's not that+형용사 그렇게 …하지 않다

658
It's not that.
그런 건 아냐.

659
It's not too late to let it go and start over.
잊어버리고 새로 시작하기에 늦지 않았어.
let it go 잊어버리다

660
It's now or never.
기회는 두 번 다시 오지 않을거야, 지금 아니면 안돼.

661
It's okay. It'll be up on YouTube.
괜찮아. 그거 유튜브에 올릴거야.
be up on YouTube 유튜브에 올라가다

662
It's on me.
내가 낼게, 내가 쏠게.
It's on the house (가게) 이건 서비스입니다

663
It's on the tip of my tongue.
혀 끝에서 뱅뱅도네, 생각이 날듯 말듯해.

664
It's out of my hands.
내 손을 떠났어, 나도 어쩔 수 없어.
Sth is out of sb's hands …의 손을 떠난 일이다, …는 어쩔 수가 없다

665
It's out of your league.
그건 네 능력 밖이야.
be (way) out of one's league …에 비해 수준이 넘 높아, 과분하다

666
It's possible to work your way to the top.
일을 열심히 해서 최고가 되는 것은 가능해.
work one's way to[toward] 노력하여 성취하다

667
It's quite a scam you got going.
그건 네가 벌이고 있는 큰 사기야.
~ sth you got going (on) 현재 네가 벌이고 있는 것

668
It's really getting to me.
그것 때문에 정말 화나, 정말 신경질 나 죽겠어.
get to sb …을 신경쓰게 하다, 거슬리게 하다, 화나게 하다

669
It's refreshing to get away for a while.
잠시 벗어나 있는 것도 재충전이 돼.

I need to get away 바람 좀 쐬어야겠어

670
It's so sad that he made a fool of her.
슬픈 일이야. 걔를 바보로 만들다니.

make a fool (out) of …을 기만하다, 바보취급하다 = fool sb = make fun of

671
It's starting to rain. That will make it easy to get a cab. **비가 오잖아. 택시 잡기가 쉽기도 하겠군.**

672
It's stuff like that.
그 비슷한거야.

673
It's the least I can do for the city I love.
내가 사랑하는 도시를 위해 내가 할 수 있는 최소한의 성의야.

It's the least I can do 최소한의 성의이다, 이 정도는 해야지

674
It's the thought that counts.
중요한 건 마음이야.

675
It's too bad you lost the contest. Nice try.
네가 떨어지다니 안됐네. 하지만 잘했어.

Nice try 시도는 좋았어

676
It's too late to start again. Period.
다시 시작하기에는 너무 늦었어. 이상, 끝.

Period 이상, 끝

677
It's very important. That's what people say.
그게 매우 중요해. 그게 바로 사람들이 하는 말이니까.

That's what people say 그게 바로 사람들이 하는 말이야

678
It's very nice of you.
정말 친절하네요.

679
It's very rude to wear a hat indoors. I'm just saying.
실내에서 모자를 쓰는 것은 실례야. 그냥 그렇다는거야.

I'm just saying 그냥 하는 말이야

680
It's working! What did I tell you?
야 된다! 내가 뭐랬어?

What did I tell you? (거봐) 내가 뭐랬어?

681

Jack prefers women with big booties.

잭은 엉덩이가 큰 여자들을 더 좋아해.

booty 엉덩이

682

Jenna's problems come as no surprise.

제나의 문제는 별로 놀랍지도 않아.

come as no surprise 놀라지 않다

683

Jessica's being prepped for surgery.

제시카는 수술 준비를 하고 있어.

be prepped for~ …할 준비를 하다

684

John and Rosie have been an item for over a year. 존과 로지는 일년 이상 사귀고 있어.

복수명사+be an item 사귀는 사이다

685

Josh is gonna end up stuck in Taiwan half the year. 조쉬는 반년간 대만에 처박혀 있게 될거야.

be stuck with sb[sth] 원치 않은 사람과 같이 있다, 원치 않은 곳에 있다

686

Jump in if you have something to say.
뭐 말할게 있으면 어서 말해봐.

Jump in 어서 말해봐

687

Just calm down. What's going on?
침착해. 무슨 일이야?

What's going on? 무슨 일이야?

688

Just figure out a way to talk him out of it.
걜 설득해서 그걸 못하게 만들 방도를 찾아봐.

find a way to + V …할 방도를 찾다(= figure out a way to+V)

689

Just go with it.
그냥 그렇게 해.

go with sth …로 하다, 선택하다, 결정하다

690

Just hold the fort for your parents.
네 부모님 대신해서 일을 봐줘.

hold the fort for sb …대신 일을 봐주다

691

Just keep in mind we haven't enough time.
시간이 충분하지 않다는 것을 명심해.

keep in mind 마음에 새기다, 명심하다

692

Just make sure you hit hard enough to leave a mark. 자국이 남도록 심하게 확실히 때리도록 해.

be hit hard 강한 타격을 받다

693

Just my luck! The show's already over.
내가 그렇지 뭐! 공연이 벌써 끝났네.

694

Just one more question. What do you do for a living? 질문 하나 더요. 하시는 일이 뭔지요?

What do you do (for a living)? 직업이 뭐야? = What is it you do?

695

Just own up to it.
그 실수한 것을 그냥 인정해.

own up to~ 잘못한 것을 인정하다

696

Just put me out of my misery.
속 편하게 알려줘.

put sb out of sb's misery 듣고 싶은 말을 해서 편하게 해주다

697
Just so we're clear, I need the money in advance. 분명히 말해두는데, 난 선불이 필요해.

just so we're clear, 분명히 말해두는데.

698
Just so you know, it's going to rain this afternoon. 그냥 말하는건데, 오늘 오후에 비올거래.

just so you know, 그냥 말해두는건데.

699
Just suck it up. You'll have a chance for promotion soon. 그냥 참아. 곧 승진기회가 올거야.

suck it up 참고 지내다, 분발하다 suck up to sb 아부하다

700
Just try me.
나한테 한번 (얘기) 해봐, 기회를 한번 줘봐.

701
Just wait and you'll get your say.
기다리면 말할 기회가 있을거야.

get[have] your say 말할 기회를 얻다

702
Keep asking him out. Don't take no for an answer. 계속 데이트 신청해. 거절해도 끝까지 밀어붙여.

Don't take no for an answer 끝까지 밀어붙여

703
Keep in touch, okay?
연락하고 지내자, 알았지?

keep[stay] in touch (with sb) 연락을 하고 지내다

704
Keep it up. You might get lucky.
계속 열심히 해. 운이 따를 수도 있으니 말야.

Keep it up 계속 열심히 해

705
Keep reading. What does it say?
계속 읽어. 뭐라고 되어 있어?

What does it say? 뭐라고 적혀 있어?

706
Keep your eye on her.
걔를 잘 지켜봐.

707
Keep your mouth shut, I owe you one.
비밀로 해줘, 내 신세졌어.

I owe you one 신세 많이 졌어

708
Knock it off.
그만해, 귀찮게 굴지마.

709

Knock yourself out. It won't be easy.
해보려면 해봐. 쉽지는 않을거야.

Knock yourself out! 맘대로 해봐!, 해보려면 해봐!

SCREEN TIPS

품사를 넘나드는 단어들

[명 → 동]
- **border** 거의 …라고 할 수 있다
- **inch** 조금씩 움직이다
- **party** (파티에서) 신나게 놀다
- **book** 예약하다
- **number** 열거하다
- **ground** 외출금지시키다
- **man** 배치시키다

[동 → 명]
- **bite** 한입거리, 먹을 것
- **get a say in** …에 대해 말할 권리가 있다
- **on the go** 계속하여, 끊임없이
- **a good buy** 싸게 산 물건
- **do and don't** 해야 할 일과 하지 말아야 할 일

[형, (부) → 동]
- **quiet** 조용해지다, 진정시키다

- **shy away from** …을 피하다
- **brave** …에 용감하게 맞서다
- **down** …을 쭉 들이키다, 마시다
- **forward** …앞으로 회송하다

[접속사 → 명]
- **ifs and buts** 변명, 구실
- **Not so many buts, please.** '그러나'라고 말하지 말게.
- **the hows and the whys** 방법과 이유

[기타]
- **solid** [형 → 부] 완전히, 가득히
- **walk** [자동 → 타동] walk 다음에 목적어가 나오면 「…를 산책시키다, 걸어서 바래다 주다」라는 뜻의 타동사가 된다.

Check it Out!
문장속에서 확인해보기!

A: How could you do something like that?
B: I won't do that again. **I promise you.**
A: How can I be sure?

A: 어떻게 그럴 수가 있어?
B: 다신 안그럴게. 약속해.
A: 그걸 어떻게 믿어?

I won't~
won't는 will not~의 축약형으로 발음은 /wount/로 해야 한다. want와는 달리 발음해야 한다.

A: I just got a call saying that my grandfather has died.
B: **I'm sorry to hear that.** Is there anything I can do for you?

A: 좀 전에 우리 할아버지께서 돌아가셨다는 전화를 받았어.
B: 그것 참 안됐구나. 내가 해줄 수 있는 일 없니?

get a call saying that~
…라고 말하는 전화를 받다. a call~ 다음에 바로 ~ing를 붙여서 전화내용을 말하는 표현법.

A: We're going out to dinner now. Would you like to join us?
B: Sure, **if you don't mind**.

A: 지금 저녁 먹으러 나갈 건데, 우리랑 같이 갈래?
B: 그래, 너희만 괜찮다면.

Sure
회화에서 대답으로 Sure를 쓰면 이는 Yes와 같은 의미로 생각하면 된다. 또한 It sure is~형태로도 쓰이는데 이 때는 부사로 '정말'이라는 강조어로 쓰인 경우이다.

A: I've finally found the perfect boyfriend.
B: I'm happy for you. Why don't you give me all of the details?

A: 나 드디어 완벽한 남자친구를 만났어.
B: 어머 정말 잘됐다. 자세히 좀 말해봐.

I've finally found~
find는 여기서처럼 뭔가 '찾다'라는 뜻이며, 뒤에 out을 붙여서 find out하게 되면 새로운 사실을 알게 되는 것을 말한다.

A: This is the nicest resort I've ever been to. **It couldn't be better.**
B: Yeah, the staff is really friendly and the food is great too.

A: 이 휴양지가 지금까지 가본 곳 중 제일 멋져. 더할 나위없군.
B: 그러게, 직원들은 정말 친절하고 음식도 근사하고 말야.

friendly
명사+ly는 잘 모르는 경향이 있다. 명사의 성질을 담고 있는 '…한'이라는 형용사가 된다. 한 예로 manly는 '남자다운'이라는 뜻이 된다.

A: **I'm talking to you!** Answer me!
B: I'm not going to answer until you show me some respect.

A: 내 말 좀 잘 들어! 대답을 하라구!
B: 절 존중하고 있다는 걸 보여주기 전까진 대답 못해요.

not~until
문법에서나 배울 줄 알았지만 실제 회화에서 많이 쓰인다. 해석은 until~ 이하를 해야지 not~이하를 하겠다고 하면 된다.

memo

후다닥 스크린영어
대표문장 2500

001

Leave it to me to find her.
걔 찾는 건 내게 맡겨.

Leave it to me 내게 맡겨 Leave it to me to+V …하는 것은 내게 맡겨

002

Leave me alone. Get off me!
날 내버려 둬. 날 놓아달라고!

Get off (of) me! 날 놓아줘! Get it off! 놔!(누가 머리를 채고 있을 때)

003

Let go of me, you pervert! You're hurting me!
놔줘, 이 변태야! 아프다고!

let go of~ 놓아주다, 해고하다

004

Let him off the hook. Show a little kindness.
걜 좀 봐줘. 친절을 좀 베풀라고.

let sb off the hook 봐주다, 놓아주다

005
Let it go.
그냥 잊어버려, 그냥 놔둬, 신경 꺼.

006
Let me ask you something. Was he better than me?
하나 물어보자. 걔가 나보다 나았어?

Let me ask you something[a question] 뭐 좀 물어볼게

007
Let me break it down for you.
내가 그거 설명해줄게.

008
Let me get back to you (on that).
나중에 이야기할게, 나중에 전화할게.

009
Let me get that for you. In you go.
제가 열어드릴게요. 안으로 들어가세요.

Let me get that for you 제가 할게요, 제가 문열어 드릴게요

010
Let me get this straight.
이건 분명히 해두자, 얘기를 정리해보자고.

011

Let me know if that book turns up.
그 책이 나왔는지 내게 알려줘.

turn up 예정된 장소에 오다, 나타나다, 소리 등을 키우다

012

Let me put it another way.
달리 말해볼게.

put (it) another way 달리 표현하다

013

Let me see. I think it was about five months ago.
그러니까. 5개월 전인 것 같아.

Let me see 뭐랄까, 어디보자 Let me see sth …을 보여줘

014

Let me sleep on it.
곰곰이 생각해봐야겠어, 하룻밤 더 생각해볼게.

sleep on 좀 더 생각해보다

015

Let me tell you something. Your girlfriend isn't cute.
말할게 있는데. 네 애인 안 귀여워.

Let me tell you something 내 말 좀 들어봐, 내 말할게 있어

016

Let me think about it.
생각 좀 해볼게.

017
Let that[this, it] be a lesson to you.
그 이야기를 교훈 삼아라.

018
Let us keep trying as long as we can.
할 수 있는 한 우리는 계속 노력해보자.
as long as~ …하는 한

019
Let's all get together and kick his ass!
모두 함께 모여서 걔를 혼내주자!
kick one's ass …을 혼내주다 = get one's ass kicked, kick ass 멋지다

020
Let's be patient. See what happens.
인내심을 갖자고. 어떻게 되는지 지켜보자고.
We'll see what happens 어떻게 되는지 보자고 = We'll see how we go

021
Let's call it a day and get some beer.
그만하고 맥주 좀 먹자.
call it a day 퇴근하다 = call it quits

022
Let's chip in to buy her dinner tonight.
돈을 조금씩 모아서 오늘 밤에 걔한테 저녁을 사주자.
chip in 갹출하다, (돈, 도움 등을) 모아서 주다(pitch in)

023
Let's do that.
그렇게 하자.

024
Let's do this again sometime.
조만간 다시 한번 모이자.

Let's do it again 또 만나자

025
Let's get going. It's really late.
출발하자. 정말 늦었어.

We'd better get going 우리 가봐야 돼 Let's get going 자 가자

026
Let's get it on!
자 시작하자!

get it on 시작하다, 섹스하다 get on = be successful

027
Let's get out of here. We got what we came for. 그만 여기서 나가자. 우린 얻고자 하는 것을 얻었어.

get what we came for 얻고자 하는 것을 얻다

028
Let's get together (sometime).
조만간 한번 보자.

029
Let's go out for a lunch break, whaddya say?
점심먹으러 나가자, 어때?

What do you say? 어때? What do you say to that? 그거 어때?

030
Let's go with this one.
이걸로 하자.

go with는 선택하다라는 뜻이다.

031
Let's grab a bite.
좀 먹자, 뭐 좀 먹으러 가자.

grab[take] a bite (to eat) 간단히 먹다, 간단히 요기하다

032
Let's head off to the new bar on our street.
우리 동네에 새로 생긴 술집으로 가자구.

head off to + N …로 향해 가다

033
Let's hit the road.
출발하자고.

034
Let's just agree to disagree on this matter.
이 문제에 대해서 서로 의견이 다르다는걸 인정하자.

agree to disagree 이견이 있음을 인정하다

035
Let's just call it even.
비긴 셈치자.

call it even 비긴 셈치다

036
Let's just play it by ear.
(그때그때) 상황에 맞게 행동하자.

037
Let's just say busy and leave it at that.
바쁘다고 하고 그만 하자.

leave it at that 그만두다, 더 이상 말하지 않다

038
Let's make a run for it.
빨리 피하자.

make a run for it 필사적으로 달아나다, 도망가다

039
Let's make fun of the hung-over naked guy.
술이 덜 깨고 다 벗은 남자를 놀려먹자.

hang over 숙취   hung-over 숙취 상태인

040
Let's move on.
다음으로 넘어가자고.

move on 담으로 넘어가자, 잊다

041
Let's move our date up to seven o'clock.
우리 데이트를 7시로 앞당기자.

move ~ up to 일정을 당기다

042
Let's not add insult to injury.
상황을 더 나쁘게 만들지는 맙시다.

to add insult to injury 상황을 더 나쁘게 만들다

043
Let's not get ahead of ourselves.
너무 앞서가지 말자.

get ahead of~ …을 앞서가다   get ahead of oneself 섣부르게 판단하다

044
Let's see what we got here.
어떤 상황인지 보자.

045
Let's see. Looks good on you.
어디보자. 네게 잘 어울려.

look good on sb …에게 어울리다 ↔ look terrible on sb …에게 안 어울리다

046
Let's take a look at it. Nice going.
저것 좀 봐봐. 참 잘했어.

Nice going! 잘했어!

047

Let's take a stand.
우리 맞서자.

take a stand 맞서다, 지키다

048

Level with me.
솔직히 말해봐.

level with sb …에게 솔직하게 얘기하다

049

Life is all about making choices.
인생은 선택들을 하는 것에 다름 아니야.

It's all about~ …가 가장 중요해

050

Like this? Am I doing it correctly?
이렇게? 내가 제대로 하고 있는거야?

Like this? 이렇게 하면 돼?, 이것처럼?

051

Likewise, and thanks again for letting me stay here.
마찬가지야. 그리고 여기 머물게 해줘서 다시 한번 고마워.

Likewise 나도 마찬가지야

052

Listen to yourself.
멍청한 소리 그만해.

053
Listen, buddy, we're just looking out for you.
들어봐, 이 친구야, 우린 널 보살펴 주려는 것뿐이야.

054
Look at 'em, look at how happy they are.
쟤들을 봐, 얼마나 행복해하고 있는지 보라구.

055
Look at you!
(감탄) 얘 좀 봐라!, (비난) 얘 좀 봐!

056
Look out! The baseball is coming toward you!
조심해! 야구공이 네게 날라와!
Look out! 조심해!

057
Look who's got game.
너 정말 잘하네.
got game …을 잘하다, 능숙하다

058
Look who's here. Do a little shopping, ladies?
이게 누구야. 쇼핑 좀 하시나요, 숙녀분들?
Look who's here! 이게 누구야!

059
Look who's talking.
사돈 남말하네.

060
Looks like that relationship is on the ropes.
걔네들 사이는 궁지에 몰린 것처럼 보여.

be on the ropes 죽을 맛이다 get sb on the ropes …을 궁지에 몰아넣다

061
Love does that to you sometimes.
사랑은 때때로 네게 그렇게 해.

do that 그렇게 하다

062
Lucky for you.
다행이다, 잘됐다.

063
Lucky me! Oh my God! That is good news!
내가 운좋네! 맙소사! 좋은 소식야!

Lucky me 내가 운좋네 = Lucky for me Lucky you 너 운좋다 = Lucky for you

064

Make it two. It's very healthy to eat salads.

같은 걸로 2개 줘요. 샐러드를 먹는게 건강에 아주 좋아요.

Make that[it] two 같은 걸로 2개 주세요

065

Make sure I don't get tied down.

내가 얽매이지 않도록 확실히 해.

tie a girl down …을 내 여자로 만들다 get tied down 얽매이다

066

May I just say again that I did not sleep with her. 난 그녀와 자지 않았다고 다시 말해도 될까요.

sleep with sb …와 섹스하다

067

May I take this as a "yes?"

이걸 승낙한 걸로 받아들여도 돼?

take that as a "yes" 승낙으로 알다

068
Maybe some other time.
다음을 기약하지.

069
Maybe we should take a break.
우리 좀 쉬자.
take a break 잠시 쉬다

070
Maybe your resolution is to not make fun of your friends.
네 다짐이라면 친구들을 놀리지 않겠다는거겠지 뭐.
make fun of …을 놀리다

071
Mike? It's me. Are you decent?
마이크? 난데. 들어가도 되겠니?
He's decent 옷을 입고 있어 Are you decent? 들어가도 돼?

072
Mind if I join you?
내가 껴도 돼?

073
Mind your own business!
상관마!, 신경꺼!, 네 일이나 신경써!

074
Most marriages even out after a few years.
대부분의 결혼은 몇 년이 지나면 잠잠해진다.

even out 안정을 찾다, 잠잠해지다

075
Mum's the word.
입 꼭 다물고 있어.

076
My boss let him go.
우리 사장이 그 사람을 해고시켰어.

let sb go 자르다, 해고하다

077
My days are all planned out.
매일 할 일이 정해져 있어.

be all planned out 모든게 계획되어져 있다

078
My mother's birthday is coming up.
내 어머니 생일이 곧 다가와.

be coming up …가 다가오다

079
My phone has been ringing off the hook.
전화가 끊임없이 왔어.

ring off the hook 전화기가 불통나다   give sb a ring = give sb a call

080

Need your cigarette lit? Allow me.
라이터 필요해요? 여기요.

Allow me 제가 할게요

081

Never mind what I want. What do you want?
내가 원하는 건 신경쓰지마. 넌 뭘 원해?

Never mind+N[~ing/S+V] …을 신경쓰지마

082

Never mind, I don't want to know.
신경쓰지마. 알고 싶지 않아.

Never mind! 신경쓰지마!

083

Nice going. You ruined my whole day.
자~알 한다. 나의 하루를 온통 망쳐놨어.

084

No disrespect here, but, um, this is total shit.
기분나쁘게 하려는 것은 아니지만 이건 정말 엉망예요.

total shit 완전 엉망

085

No hard feelings (on my part).
악의는 아냐, 기분 나쁘게 생각마.

086
No harm (done).
손해본건 없어, 잘못된 거 없어, 괜찮아.

087
No offense.
악의는 없었어, 기분 나빠하지마.

088
No offense, but I've got work to do.
기분 나빠하지마, 하지만 나 일해야 돼.

No offense, but~ 기분나빠하지마, 하지만~

089
No one can see us doing it from the parking lot.
아무도 주차장에서 우리가 섹스하는걸 볼 수가 없어.

do it 섹스하다

090
No one likes it now, but it will have its time.
지금은 아무도 그걸 좋아하지 않지만, 잘 나갈 때가 있을거야.

have its time 다 때가 있다

091
No problem at all. I'll talk to you then.
전혀 상관없어. 그럼 그때 얘기하자.

No problem at all 전혀 문제없어, 괜찮고 말고

092
No problem, I'm good to go.
괜찮아, 난 준비가 다 되어 있어.

I'm good to go 순조롭다, 준비가 다 되었어

093
No problem. I'll call back later.
괜찮아요. 나중에 다시 전화하죠.

No problem 문제없어, 괜찮아, 그럼요, 뭘

094
No question about it.
의문의 여지가 없어, 확실해.

095
No strings attached.
아무런 조건없이.

096
No thank you. I'm not in the mood.
고맙지만 됐어. 그럴 기분이 아냐.

I'm not in the mood 그럴 기분 아냐

097
No way! I'd never do something like that!
절대 아냐! 난 그런 건 절대 안해.

098
No way!
절대 안돼!, 말도 안돼!

099
No wonder.
당연하지.

100
No worries, we'll try again later.
걱정마, 나중에 다시 할거야.

No worries는 No problem처럼 자신이 알아서 할테니 "걱정마," "괜찮아" 라는 뜻이 된다.

101
No, not even after throwing the kitchen sink at it. **아니, 거기에 모든 방법을 써본 후에 조차도 안됐어.**

throw the kitchen sink 모든 방법을 강구하다

102
No. I'm looking for a hookup.
아니. 난 그냥 가벼운 만남을 원해.

hookup 만남

103
Nobody knows what life has in store.
인생은 어떻게 될지 아무도 몰라.

104

None of your business. Take it or leave it.
네 알바아니냐. 하든 말든.

Take it or leave it 하던지 말던지 해

105

Not a big leap to lying.
거짓말과 같은 셈이야.

not a big leap to~ …와 거의 마찬가지인 셈이다

106

Not a chance!
절대 안돼!, 어림없는 소리!

107

Not again! This happened a few months ago!
또 야! 몇 달전에도 그랬는데!

Not again! 어휴, 또야! 어떻게 또 그럴 수 있어!

108

Not even close.
어림도 없어.

109

Not my problem.
상관없어, 내 알 바 아니지.

110
Not right now, thanks.
지금은 됐어요, 지금은 아냐.

111
Not that I know of.
내가 알기로는 그렇지 않아.

112
Not that I can recall.
내 기억으로는 없어.

113
Not that way!
그런 식으론 안돼!

114
Not to worry.
걱정 안 해도 돼.

115
Not to worry, we're making good progress.
걱정마, 우린 많이 나아가고 있어.

Not to worry하면 상대방에게 "걱정안해도 된다"고 안심시키는 표현

116

Not to worry. I'll take care of it.
걱정마. 내가 처리할게.

take care of sth 처리하다, 지불하다(get the bill)

117

Now eat up, we have the fish course coming.
어서 먹어, 생선이 나올 차례야.

eat up은 동사구로 「어서 다 먹어치우다」라는 의미의 표현이다. 상대방에게 음식을 어서 먹으라고 권유할 때 사용한다.

118

Now go get changed because everybody's ready. 다들 준비하고 있으니 가서 옷 갈아 입어.

get changed 옷을 갈아입다

119

Now I don't feel so bad about beating you.
널 이기니 기분이 그리 나쁘지 않네.

feel so bad[good] 기분이 나쁘다[좋다]

120

Now remember, you are the bee's knees.
기억해둬, 네가 최적임자야.

the bee's knees 최적임자, 최상급의 것

121
Now take it from the top.
이제 처음부터 다시 해보자.

take it from the top (공연) 처음부터 다시 하다

122
Now that you mention it.
말이 나온 김에, 말을 하니까 말인데요, 얘기가 나와서 그런데...

123
Now you're talking!
그래 바로 그거야!, 그렇지!

124
Now you've taken on Jessica. I don't know what to say.
이제 제시카를 책임진다고 하니 뭐라고 해야 할지 모르겠어.

take on 책임지다, 맞서다

SCREEN TIPS

이상한 사람들
- **loser** 못난 놈, 인생의 낙오자, 형편없는 사람
- **weirdo** 괴짜(역시 형용사+-o의 형태로 weird는 「이상야릇한」, 「기묘한」이라는 뜻)
- **nerd** 공부벌레, 얼간이, 공부만 하거나 사교성이 부족한 사람
- **jerk** 바보, 얼간이 [머리가 나쁘다기 보다 세상 물정에 어둡고 말하는 사람의 맘에 들지 않는 사람에게 쓰는 말로, 비슷한 표현으로는 schmuck, slob 등이 있다]
- **geek** 멍청하고 좀 이상한 놈 [cf. geeky 이상한, 괴짜같은]
- **dork** 띨한 놈, 멍청한 놈 [학생들이 많이 사용 / cf. dorky 멍청한]
- **You bastard!** 나쁜 자식! [「사생아」라는 뜻에서 출발한 욕설로 주로 화가 머리끝까지 난 여성들이 남성에게 즐겨 사용]
- **moron** 바보
- **creep** 꼴보기 싫은 놈, 괴짜
- **douch bag** 얼간이
- **freak** 괴상망칙한 놈, 뭔가에 병적으로 집착하는 사람
- **skank** 더러운 놈
- **scum** 인간 쓰레기

125

Oh God, he's really bleeding. Get a doctor!
맙소사, 피가 많이 흐르네. 의사 불러!

Get a doctor! 의사를 불러와!

126

Oh, a pepperoni pizza! That's what I'm talking about. **어, 페페로니 피자! 내가 말한게 바로 그거야.**

That's what I'm talking about 내 말이 바로 그거야

127

Oh, by the way, you should pop over and meet her. **그건 그렇고 넌 잠시 가서 걜 만나봐.**

pop out 잠시 외출하다, 나가다 pop by 잠시 들리다 pop over 잠시 오다

128

Oh, don't get me wrong. I'm good.
어, 오해하지마. 난 괜찮아.

I'm good 난 괜찮아, (거절하면서) 됐어 good for+시간 …시간이 괜찮다

129

Oh, forget it. It's not that important.
저기 잊어버려. 그리 중요한 것도 아냐.

Forget it 잊어버려, 신경쓰지마

130

Oh, fuck! Oh, fuck! God damn it!
어, 빌어먹을! 젠장! 제기랄!

단독으로 Fuck!하게 되면 자기 뜻대로 일이 안풀리거나 기분 나쁠 때 사용하면 된다.

131

Oh, just piss off, will you?
그냥 꺼져 줄래?

Piss off! 꺼져! piss off sb 화나게 하다

132

Oh, my God, this can't be happening.
맙소사, 이런 일이 있을 수가.

This can't be happening! 이럴 리가 없어! = I can't believe this is happening

133

Oh, my God. What have you done?
오, 맙소사. 너 무슨 짓을 한거야?

What have you done? 너 무슨 짓을 한거야?

134

On what grounds?
무슨 증거로?, 무슨 근거로?

135
One way or another.
어떻게든 해서.

136
Ooh, booty call? I can take a walk around the block if you want. 섹스하자는 전화야? 원하면 밖에서 산책할게.
booty call 조건없이 섹스하자는 전화

137
Our date was boring, apart from going to a nightclub. 우리 데이트는 나이트클럽에 간거 빼고는 지루했어.
apart from ~ing …을 제외하고, …뿐만 아니라

138
Our honeymoon will take place in June.
신혼여행은 6월에 가게 될거야.
take place 일어나다, 생기다

139
Our relationship? That's history.
우리 관계? 다 지난 일이야.
That[It] is history 다 지난 일야

140
Out of all that, that's all you got?
그 많은 것 중에서 생각하는게 고작 그거야?
That's all you got 고작 그것 뿐이야

141

Over my dead body! Those things are dangerous. 죽어도 안돼! 그런 건 너무 위험해.

Over my dead body! 절대 안돼!

142

Pardon me for stepping on your foot.
발을 밟아서 죄송해요.

Pardon me (for) 죄송해요

143

Pardon my French[language, expression].
욕설해서 미안.

Pardon 대신에 Excuse를 써도 된다.

144

Pardon? You'll need to speak louder.
뭐라구요? 좀 크게 말해주세요.

Pardon? 다시 말해주세요

145

People actually do that?
사람들이 실제로 그렇게 해?

146

Place your bet over there at that table.
저기 저 테이블에서 내기를 해봐.

place one's bet 내기를 걸다

147
Play it cool and everything will be OK.
침착히 행동하면 다 잘 될거야.

play it cool 침착하다

148
Please don't act like a selfish fucking bitch!
이기적인 못된 년처럼 행동하지마!

fucking은 아주 강조하고 싶은 단어 앞에 붙이기만 하면 된다.

149
Please don't be upset, it could happen to anyone.
화내지마, 그럴 수도 있는 일이야.

It could happen 그럴 수도 있다 It just happened 어쩌다 그렇게 됐어

150
Please don't give me a hard time.
제발 날 힘들게 하지마.

give sb a hard time …을 힘들게 대하다

151
Please get your hands off my breasts!
내 가슴에서 손 좀 치워!

keep[take, get] one's hands off (of) ~ …에서 손을 떼다, 건드리지 않다

152
Please stop bugging me.
나 좀 귀찮게 하지마.

153

Please, for the love of God, get me out of it!

빌어먹을, 제발 날 꺼내줘!

154

Point well taken.

무슨 말인지 잘 알았어.

155

Problem solved. Welcome aboard.

문제 해결됐어. 함께 일하게 된 걸 환영해.

Welcome aboard 탑승을 환영합니다, 함께 일하게 되어 기뻐

156

Promise me you'll stand by Andrew.

앤드류를 지지해준다고 약속해.

stand by …을 지원하다, 지지하다

157

Pull over right here.

바로 여기에 차를 세워요.

pull over 길가에 차를 세우다, 차를 옆으로 대다 pull up (신호등 등에) 차를 세우다

158

Put yourself out there.

당당하고 자신있게 나서봐.

put oneself out there 자신있게 나서다

159

Remember who you are.

네가 누구인지 기억해라.

160

Right back at ya.

너도 그래, 너와 동감이야.

161

Right off the top of my head, I'd say your plan won't succeed. 지금 막 드는 생각으로는 네 계획이 성공 못할 것 같아.

(It is) (right) Off the top of my head 깊이 생각해보지 않고 바로, 감으로 대충, 즉석에서

162

Ron was retired by the time you came on the job. 론은 네가 들어왔을 때쯤 퇴직했어.

by the time~ …할 때쯤

163

Room all clear! Check him!

방 모두는 이상없어! 저 사람만 확인해봐!

Clear! (수색하면서) 이상없음!

S

164

Sam is proposing, she'll lose it and they'll break up. 샘이 프로포즈를 한다는데, 걔가 화를 낼거고 그럼 헤어질거야.

lose one's shit 화를 내다, 열광하다 lose it 화내다, 미치다

165

Sam knew her way around this town.
샘은 이 마을지리를 꽤 잘 알아.

know one's way around 잘 알고 있다

166

Sam really is off her game.
샘은 정말 제 컨디션이 아냐.

be off the game 컨디션이 안좋다 have taken ill 병에 걸리다

167

Sam was sacked for speaking his mind at the meeting. 샘은 회의에서 속내 이야기를 해서 잘렸어.

be[get] sacked 잘리다, 해고당하다 = be fired

168
Same as always. He's still healthy.
여전하셔. 아직도 건강하셔.

as always 언제나처럼

169
Say no more. I know it's your daughter's birthday.
알겠어. 딸 생일이지.

Say no more 더 말 안해도 알아, 무슨 말인지 말 안 해도 알겠어

170
Say what?
뭐라고?, 다시 말해줄래?

171
Says here Dr. Smith examined him last week.
지난주에 스미스 박사가 걜 검사했다고 되어있어.

It says ~ …라고 적혀 있어, …라고 되어 있어

172
Screw you, you ungrateful bitch!
엿먹어, 이 은혜도 모르는 년아!

Screw sb[sth]! 꺼져!, 집어쳐!

173
See what I'm saying?
무슨 말인지 알지?

174

Seriously? You thought that was a good idea?
정말? 그게 좋은 생각이라고 여겼어?

Seriously? 정말로, 정말 이럴거야?, 너무 하네

175

Seriously? You've never done this before?
정말? 이거 해본 적이 없다고?

You've never done this before? 이거 해본 적 없어?

176

Shame on you!
부끄러운 줄 알아야지!, 창피한 일이야!

177

She acts like we didn't kiss. It's like it never happened.
걘 우리가 키스 안한 것처럼 행동해. 마치 없었던 일처럼.

It's like it never happened 없었던 일처럼 잊어버리다(잊거나 용서하거나)

178

She didn't come here. Not that I know of.
걘 여기로 오지 않았어. 내가 알고 있는 한.

Not that I know of 내가 알기로는 그렇지 않아

179

She didn't leave yet. Not that I'm aware of.
걘 아직 떠나지 않았어. 내가 알기로는 아냐.

Not that I'm aware of 내가 알기로는 아냐

180
She flipped for the guy she met online.
걘 온라인에서 만난 남자를 무척 좋아했어.

flip for~ 좋아하기 시작하다, 무척 좋아하다

181
She has a college tour coming up.
조만간 걘 대학순방을 하게 될거야.

have sth coming up …가 다가오다

182
She has always thought she's hot shit.
걔는 자기가 거물이라고 항상 생각해.

hot shit 잘했어, 거물 don't know shit 아무것도 모르다

183
She has been giving me the eye.
그녀는 날 눈독들이고 있었어.

give sb the eye 눈독들이다 lay eyes on 눈길주다, 눈독들이다

184
She has it in for me.
걘 날 싫어해.

have it in for sb …에게 원한을 품다, 싫어하다

185
She insists on doing it all herself.
걘 혼자 다 하겠다고 고집을 펴.

insist on~ …을 고집하다

186
She is going to classes to prepare for the delivery. 그 여자는 출산 준비를 위한 강좌에 다닐거야.

187
She is just in a bad mood this evening.
걘 오늘 저녁 그냥 기분이 안좋을뿐야.
be in good[bad] mood …할 기분이다[아니다]

188
She is not marriage material.
그 여자는 결혼상대는 아냐.

189
She is on a roll.
그 여자 한창 잘나가고 있어.

190
She is on the phone trying to get hold of Jim.
걔는 짐하고 연락하려고 통화중이야.
get (a) hold of~ 연락을 취하다

191
She is schmoozing her way up the career ladder! 걘 친목으로 승진을 하고 있어!
schmooze one's way 사교로[친목으로] 나아가다

192
She is so terrible at impressions.
걔 정말 흉내를 못해.

be poor[terrible] at~ …을 잘 못하다, 서투르다

193
She is working on a crossword puzzle.
걔 크로스워드 퍼즐을 풀고 있어.

work on …에 관한 일을 하다

194
She just wouldn't take no for an answer.
걔는 받아들이지 않으려고 해.

wouldn't take no for an answer 끝까지 받아들이지 않으려 하다

195
She keeps herself busy with her kids.
그녀는 아이들로 바빠.

keep oneself busy[occupied]~ …하느라 바쁘다

196
She left word with my parents.
걔 우리 부모님에게 메시지를 남겼어.

leave word(s) with sb …에게 메시지를 남기다

197
She plans to go away during her summer vacation. 걔는 여름휴가 때 놀러갈 계획이야.

go away 자리를 뜨다(leave), (휴가 등으로) 멀리 놀러가다

198

She probably got him worked up into it.

개는 그를 부추겨서 그것을 하게 했을거야.

get sb worked up into~ …을 부추겨 …하게 하다

199

She pulls this funny face during sex like this.

걘 섹스할 때 이처럼 이상한 표정을 지어.

pull the funny face 이상한 표정을 짓다   pull[make] a face 인상을 쓰다

200

She put me up to it.

걔가 선동해서 그 짓을 하게 된거야.

put sb up to sth …에게 (멍청한 짓)을 하도록 부추키다

201

She said we must move, or words to that effect. 걘 우리가 이사해야 된대, 뭐 그런 얘기였어.

~, or words to that effect 뭐 그런 얘기였어

202

She seems to like me. I'm so in there.

걔가 나를 좋아하는 것 같아. 일이 잘 풀렸어.

I'm so in there 일이 잘 풀렸어

203

She showed up, that's what.

걔가 나타났고 그래서 그렇게 된거야.

~that's what 그래서 그렇게 된거야

204

She started freaking out on me, so I backed off. 걔가 내게 기겁하길래 내가 물러섰어.

be freaking out 놀라다, 기겁하다 *be going to freak out의 형태로 쓰인다

205

She stood guard over the money she found.

걔는 자기가 발견한 돈을 지키고 있었어.

stand[keep] guard over~ …을 지켜보다, 지켜주다, 보호하다

206

She was all over me. She kissed me.

그녀는 내게 들이대면서 키스를 했어.

be all over sb …을 완전히 잊다, 애무하면서 들이대다

207

She was really nice to me even though I'm such a loser. 내가 이렇게 못난 놈인데도 그 여자는 내게 정말 잘해줬어.

208

She was trying to make up with you.

걘 너와 화해하려고 했어.

make up (with sb) 화해하다

209

She will wind up with her heart broken or pregnant. 걘 상처받거나 임신하게 될거야.

wind up with[in, at] …한 상태에 놓치다 = wind up ~ing

210
She works really hard every day. I like that.
걘 정말 매일 열심히 일해. 맘에 들어.

I love[like] that 좋아, 맘에 들어

211
She wrote a book? No kidding?
걔가 책을 썼다고? 정말?

No kidding 설마?, 이제야 알았어?, 진심이야, 맞아, 그렇지

212
She'd be a good match for Jeremy.
걔는 제레미와 아주 잘 어울릴거야.

be a good match for~ 잘 어울리다 ↔ be not a good match for~

213
She'll see through it.
그녀가 속셈을 눈치챌거야.

see through~ 꿰뚫어보다, 속셈을 눈치채다

214
She's a beauty. I can't deny it.
걔는 정말 미인이야. 인정해.

I can't deny it 인정할게 Don't bother deny it 그냥 인정해

215
She's a bitch. Hold out for a good girl.
걘 나쁜 년이야. 좋은 여자를 포기하지 말고 계속 찾으라고.

be a bitch 못된 년이다

216
She's a lot prettier than you let on.
걘 네가 얘기한 것보다 훨씬 예쁘더라.

spill the beans 비밀을 누설하다 let on 비밀을 말하다

217
She's always upset. I don't get her.
걘 늘상 화를 내. 이해가 안돼.

I don't get her 개가 이해가 안돼

218
She's been gagging for me to get with her.
걔는 내가 자기와 함께 데이트하기를 바라고 있어.

be gagging for~ …에 약하다, 특히 섹스를 하고 싶어하다

219
She's friends with my brother.
걔 우리 형하고 친구야.

220
She's gone and I'm left with no one.
걔는 가버렸고 난 혼자 남겨졌어.

I'm left with no one 혼자 남겨졌어

221
She's gonna mooch off us.
걔는 우리에게 빌붙어살거야.

mooch off …에게 얻어먹다, 빌붙다

222
She's got another thing coming.
걔 그러다 큰 코 다칠거야.

223
She's got her bases covered.
걘 만반의 준비를 다했어.

have all the bases covered 준비를 철저히 하다

224
She's got some breast implants. That's for sure.
쟨 가슴수술받았어. 확실해.

for sure 물론, 확실해(That's for sure)

225
She's mine for the taking.
내가 원한다면 그녀는 내꺼야.

for the taking 원한다면 맘대로

226
She's moving faster than you. Put your back into it. 걔가 당신보다 더 빨리 움직이네. 노력을 더 해봐.

put one's back into it 전력투구하다, 온 힘을 기울이다

227
She's nice, but she does a lot of talking.
걔는 착한데, 말이 너무 많아.

do a lot of talking 얘기를 많이 하다

228
She's not a knockout.
그 여자가 끝내주게 예쁜 건 아니지.
knockout 끝내주게 예쁜 사람

229
She's not good enough to raise a child.
걔는 애를 키우기에는 부족해.
Good enough! 충분해!, 그만하면 됐어! good enough for sb to+V …가 …하기에 충분해

230
She's not like I thought at all.
그녀는 내가 생각했던 것와는 전혀 달라.
be not like I thought at all 전혀 생각과 달라

231
She's not like you. She doesn't hold on to that stuff.
걘 너와 달라. 걘 그런 일에 집착하지 않아.
hold on to~ 고수하다, 매달리다

232
She's only sleeping with you to get back at me.
걘 내게 앙갚음하기 위해 너와 자는거야.
get back at[on] sb 복수하다, 앙갚음하다

233
She's quite a catch, isn't she? You like her, don't you?
걘 정말 멋져, 그렇지 않아? 너 걔 좋아하지, 그렇지?
be quite a catch 멋진 사람이다

234

She's really in touch with her artistic nature.
걔는 자신의 예술적 기질을 잘 이해하고 있어.

be[keep, stay] in touch with sth 상황 등을 잘 이해하다

235

She's really my type. I think we'll go out again.
걘 정말 내 타입야. 다시 데이트할거야.

be one's type …의 타입이다

236

She's so sexy. I'll give you that.
걘 정말 섹시해. 네 말이 맞아.

I'll give you that 네 말이 맞아, 그건 그래

237

She's very supportive.
걘 도움이 많이 되고 있어.

238

She's with us.
걘 우리 일행이야.

be with sb …는 …와 일행이다 sb be with+기관 …에서 일하다, …에서 나오다

239

Show me what you got.
네 실력을 보여줘봐.

Show me what you've got! 네 능력[실력]을 보여줘!

240

Shut the fuck up! You are a loser!
아가리 닥쳐! 넌 한심한 놈야!

Shut the fuck up! 아가리 닥쳐!

241

Shut your eyes, and go with your first instinct.
두 눈을 감고 처음 느낀 본능에 따라.

go with 선택하다(choose), 받아들이다

242

Simon was able to date two girls. Classic!
사이몬은 여자 두 명과 데이트할 수 있었어. 대단해!

Classic! 대단하군!(Great!)

243

Smoking is bad. This is not me talking. It's a scientific fact. 흡연은 안좋아. 내가 하는 말이 아니라, 과학적 사실이야.

This is not me talking 내가 하는 얘기가 아냐

244

So are we having fun?
그럼 우리 재미있게 보내고 있는거야?

be having fun 재미있게 보내다

245

So be it.
그렇게 되라지, 그래 그렇게 해, 맘대로 해.

246
So I figured it out.
그래서 (연유를) 알게 되었지.

247
So is Ben settling in okay?
그럼 벤이 적응 잘하고 있는거야?

settle in 자리잡다, 적응하다 = get settled in

248
So it seems the marriage is over.
결혼 생활은 끝이 난 것 같아.

So it seems 그런 것 같아

249
So shoot me.
그래서 어쨌다는거야?(화자의 무관심)

250
So you make love to me and then you go back to your husband?
그럼 나와 섹스하고 나서 다시 남편에게로 돌아간다는거야?

make love to sb …와 사랑을 나누다, …와 섹스하다

251
So, what's your plan B?
그 다음 계획은 뭐야?, 차선책은 뭐야?

252

So, where is this tool meant to be meeting you? 널 만나기로 되어 있던 이 녀석은 어디있는거야?

tool 자신이 멋지다고 생각하는 얼간이

253

Some reporters have been snooping around.
일부 기자들은 염탐을 하고 있어.

snoop around~ …염탐하다, 기웃거리다

254

Some students snuck out of school.
일부 학생들은 몰래 학교에서 빠져나갔어.

sneak out~ …몰래 나가다

255

Somebody better tell Tom the bad news.
누군가 탐에게 이 나쁜 소식을 말해줘야 돼.

give[tell] sb the bad news 안좋은 소식을 전하다

256

Something went wrong.
뭔가 잘못됐어.

go wrong 실수하다, 잘못되다

257

Something's come up and he can't attend our wedding. 일이 생겨서 우리 결혼식에 참석할 수가 없대.

Something's come up 일이 좀 생겼어(Something has come up)

258

Sometimes she would just play hooky and spend the day with me. 때때로, 걔는 수업을 빼먹고 나와 시간을 보내곤

spend the evening[night] with~ …와 저녁[밤]을 보내다 play hooky 학교를 빼먹다

259

Sometimes you have to take chances.
때론 위험을 감수해야 돼.

take a chance[chances] 위험부담을 감수하다 take the chance 그 기회를 잡다

260

Sorry it didn't work out, but you can't have it all. 잘 안되서 미안한데, 하지만 다 가질 수는 없잖아.

You can't have it all 다 가질 수는 없어

261

Sounds like a plan.
좋은 생각이야.

262

Sounds like a plan. I'll see you at 8:00.
좋은 생각이야. 8시에 보자고.

Sounds like a good idea 좋은 생각이야(= Sounds like a plan)

263

Spare me the details.
요점만 말해, 자세히 말하지마.

264

Speak for yourself! I really love to jog.
너나 그렇지! 난 조깅하는거 정말 좋아해.

speak for yourself하게 되면 상대방의 말에 반대하면서 "너나 그렇지," 하지만 the facts speak for themselves처럼 사물주어가 오면 「스스로 명백해지다」는 말이 된다.

265

Spend all of your money. Go big or go home.
네 돈을 다 쓰라고. 하려면 제대로 해야지.

Go big or go home 하려면 제대로 해야지

266

Stay out of this!
끼어들지마!

267

Stay out of trouble.
말썽 피지마, 문제 일으키지마.

268

Stay with me.
가지마, 침착해, (죽어가는 사람) 정신차려.

269

Stick with it. You'll make a lot of money.
포기하지마. 돈을 많이 벌거야.

stick with it 포기하지 않다, 계속하다

270

Stop beating me to the punch!
그만 좀 선수치라고!

beat sb to the punch 기선을 제압하다

271

Stop bragging about it.
제발 잘난 척 좀 그만해.

272

Stop saying that. You have to be honest with me.
그런 말마. 너 내게 솔직히 말해.

to be honest 솔직히 말해서 = to be frank with you

273

Stop yapping about your problems.
네 문제들로 수다를 그만 떨어라.

yap about 수다를 떨다 = gab about

274

Sure thing, boss. Coming right up.
물론이죠, 보스. 바로 나갑니다.

come right up 바로 나갑니다, 바로 가요

Check it Out!
문장속에서 확인해보기!

> **A:** Let me ask you something. Would it be okay with you if I <u>set Rick up on a date.</u>
> **B:** Oh, what? <u>With who?</u>

A: 뭐 좀 물어볼게. 내가 릭한테 소개팅을 시켜줘도 너 괜찮겠어?
B: 어머, 뭐라구? 누굴 소개시켜 줄 건데?

With who?

who를 whom으로 고쳐야 된다고 주장한다면 아직 살아있는 영어에 약한 경우. 문법적으로는 whom를 써야 맞지만 실제는 who로 쓴지 오래됐다.

> **A:** He's not here.
> **B:** Could I <u>leave a message</u>?
> **A:** <u>No problem.</u> What is it?

A: 그 사람 여기 없어요.
B: 메시지를 남길 수 있을까요?
A: 그럼요. 어떤 메시지인데요?

leave a message

'메시지를 남긴다'라는 뜻이고 반대로 '메시지를 받겠다'라고 하려면 take a message라고 하면 된다.

> **A:** Can I borrow your car for a date tonight?
> **B:** <u>No way!</u> Last time you borrowed it, you <u>left</u> the gas tank <u>empty</u>.

A: 오늘 밤 데이트하러 가는데 네 차 좀 빌릴 수 있을까?
B: 절대 안돼! 지난번에 빌려갔을 때 네가 기름을 몽땅 다 써버렸잖아.

leave+목적어+형용사

'…을 …한 상태로 두다'라는 5형식 구문이다. 동사가 한 형식에 얽매이지 않고 여러 형식으로 쓰이니 열린 마음으로 동사의 쓰임새를 익혀두어야 한다.

A: I wanted to know how to use this computer, so **I figured it out.**
B: Is it very useful to you?

know how to+V
how to+V라는 의문사구가 동사 know의 목적어로 쓰인 경우이다. "그거 하는 방법을 알려줘"라고 하려면 Show me how to do it이라고 하면 된다.

A: 이 컴퓨터 사용법을 알고 싶었는데 말야, 결국 알아냈다구.
B: 그게 너한테 아주 유용한 거야?

A: How did you meet Angela?
B: **She's friends with my brother.** They've known each other a long time.

a long time
for a long time은 오랫동안이라는 의미로 기간을 강조하는 반면, a long time은 그냥 '오랜 시간'을 의미한다.

A: 안젤라를 어떻게 만났어?
B: 걘 우리 형하고 친구야. 둘은 오랫동안 알고 지내왔어.

A: Are you eavesdropping?
B: Shh, they are talking about Tom and Jane.
A: **Shame on you!**

talk about~
talk은 다양한 전치사와 함께 쓰인다. talk to(…에게 이야기하다), talk with(…와 함께 이야기하다), 그리고 talk about은 …에 관해 이야기하다라는 뜻이다.

A: 너 엿듣고 있는거야?
B: 쉿, 탐하고 제인에 대해 얘기중이야.
A: 창피한 줄 알아!

memo

후다닥 스크린영어
대표문장 2500

001

Take care. And don't forget to e-mail me.

조심해. 그리고 잊지 말고 내게 이메일보내고.

Take care! 잘 지내!, 조심해! Take care of oneself! 몸 조심해!

002

Take it easy. We have a lot of time.

진정하라고. 우리 시간이 많잖아.

take it easy는 「걱정하지마」, 「좀 쉬어가면서 해」, 혹은 헤어질 때의 인사로 "잘 지내"라는 의미를 갖는다.

003

Take it from me, Mom loves you.

내 말을 믿어. 엄만 널 사랑하셔.

take it from sb …의 말을 믿다

004

Take it or leave it.

선택의 여지가 없어, 받아들이든지 말든지 알아서 해.

005

Take it up with your boss.

사장하고 이야기해봐.

take it up with sb (문제, 제안)…와 상의하다, 이야기하다

006

Take your time. There's no rush.

천천히 해. 서두르지 않아도 돼.

Take your time 서두르지마   Take it easy[slow] 천천히 해

007

Take your time. Think about it.

서두르지 말고 생각해봐.

Think about it 생각해봐

008

Talk to Chris. He knows what is what.

크리스에게 말해. 걘 다 알고 있어.

know what is what 진상을 알다

009

Ted will friend anyone that sends him a request. 테드는 요청만 하면 누구나 다 친추할거야.

friend v. SNS상에서 친구맺다

010

Tell me about it. It's so frustrating.

네 말이 맞아. 정말 실망스러워.

Tell me about it 누가 아니래, 네 말이 맞아

011
Tell me another (one).
말도 안되는 소리하지마, 거짓말마, 헛소리하지마.

012
Tell me what you're thinking.
네 생각이 뭔지 말해 봐.

013
Thank you so much for coming on such a short notice. 이렇게 갑작스럽게 찾아와주시니 감사하기 그지없군요.

on a short notice (미리 알려주지 않고) 갑작스럽게, 급하게

014
Thank you so much, Kate. You saved my life.
정말 고마워, 케이트. 너 때문에 살았어.

save one's life ⋯의 목숨을 구하다, 살려주다

015
Thanks for bringing her back in one piece.
걜 무사히 데려와줘서 고마워.

We got here in one piece 무사히 도착하다

016
Thanks for coming over. I owe you big time.
와줘서 고마워. 신세 많이 졌어.

I owe you big time 신세 많이 졌어

017
Thanks for keeping me company.
나와 말동무해줘서 고마워.
keep sb company …와 말동무하다

018
That (all) depends.
상황에 따라 달라, 경우에 따라 달라.

019
That ain't the way I heard it.
내가 듣기로는 그게 아닌데, 나는 다르게 들었는데.

020
That can't be done overnight.
저건 하룻밤 사이에 마칠 수 없는 일이야.
It can't be done 그렇게 될 수 없어, 끝낼 수 없어

021
That can't be.
뭔가 잘못된거야, 그럴 리가 없어.

022
That car is an old piece of shit.
저 차는 쓸모가 없어.
be a piece of shit[crap] 개떡같다, 쓸모없다

023
That could be the right answer. That could be it. 그게 맞는 정답일 수도 있어. 그거일 수도 있어.

That could be it 그거일 수도 있다

024
That famous singer has the world at his feet.
저 유명가수는 세상 부러울게 없어.

have the world at one's feet 세상 부러울게 없다

025
That figures. He always was very smart.
그럴 줄 알았어. 걘 항상 매우 똑똑했어.

That[It] figures 그럴 줄 알았어

026
That gives me an idea.
그러고 보니 좋은 수가 떠올랐어.

027
That goes for the rest of you!
나머지도 다 마찬가지야!

That[The same] goes for~ …도 마찬가지이다

028
That has never happened before.
난생 처음 겪는 일이야.

029
That is how it's done.
이렇게 하는거야.

030
That makes no sense at all.
그건 전혀 말도 안돼.

make no sense 말이 안된다

031
That makes sense.
일리가 있군.

032
That makes two of us. I'm in total agreement.
나도 그래. 전적으로 같은 생각이야.

That makes two of us 나도 그래, 나도 그렇게 생각해

033
That marriage is on the road to disaster.
그 결혼은 파멸의 길로 가고 있어.

be on the road to disaster 상황이 끔찍해지고 있어, 파멸로 가고 있다

034
That reminds me. I mustn't go home without him. 그러고보니 생각나네. 난 걔없이 집에 가면 안돼.

That reminds me 그러고보니 생각나네

035
That settles it. We'll work out the details later.
그럼 해결된거야. 세부사항은 나중에 해결하자고.

That settles it 그럼 해결된거야

036
That sounds delicious. I'll have the same.
맛있겠다. 나도 같은 걸로 할게.

The same for me 같은 걸로 주세요 = I'll have the same

037
That sounds great. Don't do anything I wouldn't do. 멋지네. 엉뚱한 짓 하지말고.

Don't do anything I wouldn't do 내가 하지 않을 일은 너도 하지마

038
That was close. We nearly didn't make it.
아슬아슬했어. 우리는 거의 도착하지 못할 뻔했어.

That was close 아슬아슬했어

039
That was dumb. What were you thinking?
멍청했네. 무슨 생각으로 그런거야?

What were you thinking (about)? 무슨 생각으로 그런거야?

040
That was so sweet of you to wait for me!
날 기다려줘서 정말 고마워!

That's (very) sweet of you 참 고마워라(How sweet of you)

041

That will do. You guys can go home now.
그만하면 됐어. 이제 집에 가봐.

That will do 이제 됐어, 이제 그만

042

That would be great. I really appreciate it.
그거 좋지, 정말 고마워.

I appreciate it[that] 고마워 I appreciate it that S+V …에 감사해

043

That'll teach her!
그래도 싸지!, 당연한 대가야!, 좋은 공부가 될 거야!

That'll teach sb to do …가 …하는데 도움이 될 거야

044

That's a classic. He loves pizza.
늘상 그래. 걘 피자를 아주 좋아해.

That's a classic은 "전형적이야"라는 말.

045

That's a good point.
좋은 지적이야, 맞는 말이야.

046

That's a new machine. What do you call that?
새로운 기계네. 이름이 뭐야?

What do you call that? 그걸 뭐라고 해?

> 047

That's all right. I still slept well.
괜찮아. 잠 잘 잤어.

That's right(맞아) vs. That's all right(괜찮아 = No problem)

> 048

That's all that matters.
바로 그게 중요한거야, 가장 중요한거지.

> 049

That's always the case with Jenny.
제니는 항상 그런 식이라니까.

not be always the case 항상 이러지는 않다

> 050

That's an interesting movie. What's it called?
흥미로운 영화네. 제목이 뭐였지?

What's it called? 그거 뭐라고 해?

> 051

That's another[a different] story.
그건 또 다른 얘기야, 사정이 다른 얘기야.

> 052

That's awesome for you.
너 정말 대단해.

053
That's big of you. He needs help.
착하기로 해라. 걘 도움이 필요해.

That's big of you 친절하기도 해라(How big of you)

054
That's easy for you to say.
그렇게 말하기는 쉽지, 말이야 그렇지.

055
That's enough!
이제 그만!, 됐어 그만해!

056
That's getting on my nerves.
신경 거슬려, 열받아.

get on sb's nerve …를 화나게 하다

057
That's good for you. But what's in it for me?
너한테는 좋은 일이지만 나한테는 무슨 이득이 되는데?

What's in it for sb? …가 얻는게 뭔데?

058
That's good to know. I worked very hard on it.
기쁘네요. 아주 열심히 준비했거든요.

(That's) Good to know 알게 돼서 기뻐

059
That's good. Now just keep it going, ready?
좋아. 이게 계속 돌아가게 해, 준비됐어?

Keep that going! 그거 계속 돌아가도록 해!

060
That's it? It's over? Just like that?
그게 다야? 정말 끝이란 말야? 그냥 이렇게?

Just like that? 그냥 그렇게?

061
That's it? That's all you're having?
그게 다야? 있는 게 그게 전부야?

That's it? 그게 다야?, 이게 끝이야?

062
That's just a huge burden suddenly lifted off my mind. 그건 커다란 짐을 갑자기 덜게 된 것이야.

lift off one's mind 짐을 덜다

063
That's just my luck. No boys want to date me.
내가 그렇지 뭐. 아무도 나하고 데이트 안 하려고 해.

That's just my luck 내 운이 그렇지 뭐

064
That's more like it.
그게 더 낫네, 바로 그거야.

065
That's nice.
좋아.

066
That's not exactly how it happened.
정확히 말해서 그건 그렇게 된게 아냐.
I don't know what happened 무슨 일인지 몰라

067
That's not fair! It's not our fault!
불공평해! 우리 잘못이 아니란말야!
That's not fair 공평하지 않아

068
That's not how it[this] works.
그렇게는 안돼.

069
That's not my thing.
난 그런 건 질색이야, 내 관심사 밖이야, 내 취향이 아니야.

070
That's not the point.
핵심은 그게 아니라고.

071
That's not what I mean.
실은 그런 뜻이 아니야.

072
That's really something.
정말 대단해, 거 굉장하네.

073
That's such a low blow.
그건 정말 비열한 행동이야.

low blow 비열한 행위, 치사한 짓

074
That's that. I've got some packing to do.
다 끝났어. 짐싸야겠어.

~that's that 그걸로 끝이야, 이게 전부야 That was that 일이 그렇게 된거야

075
That's the limit.
더 이상 못참아.

076
That's the thing!
그거라니까!, 그렇지!, 바로 그게 문제야!

077
That's too bad.
저런, 안됐네, 이를 어쩌나.

078
That's weird. Do you know why he did that?
거 이상하네. 걔가 왜 그랬는지 알아?

That's weird 거 참 이상하네 weirdo 이상한 사람

079
That's what I thought.
나도 그렇게 생각했어, 나도 그 생각이야.

080
That's what I wanted to hear!
그게 바로 내가 듣고 싶었던거야!

That's what we do here 여기서 우리는 바로 그렇게 해

081
That's what they all say.
다들 그렇게 말하겠지.

082
That's where I turned my life around.
바로 거기서 내 인생이 역전됐어.

083
That's where you're wrong.
바로 그 점이 네가 틀린거야.

084
That's your call.
네가 결정할 문제야, 네 뜻에 따르게.

085
The best part is that you already know everything about her!
가장 좋은 점은 네가 걔에 대해서 이미 다 알고 있다!

The best part is~ 가장 좋은 부분은 …이다

086
The best way to punish a guy is to beat him to death. 혼내는 가장 좋은 방법은 죽도록 패는거야.

beat sb to death[a pulp] 늘씬 패주다

087
The candle is on the table. Blow it out.
테이블 위에 촛불이 켜져 있어. 불어 꺼.

blow it out 불어서 끄다, 물리치다, 절연하다

088
The car almost hit me. That was a close call.
저 차가 날 거의 칠 뻔했어. 위험천만했어.

That was a close call 위험천만했어

089
The changing room is around the corner on your left. 탈의실은 모퉁이를 돌아 왼편에 있습니다.

be (just) around the corner 바로 가까이에 있다, 임박했다

090
The children's toys eat up batteries.
아이들 장난감은 배터리를 많이 잡아먹어.

Sth eat up 많이 차지하다 sth eat me up …때문에 힘들다

091
The concert was totally bitching.
콘서트가 정말이지 대단했어.

bitching 대단한, 멋진

092
The cops grilled him for four hours.
경찰은 그를 네 시간동안 다그쳤어.

grill 다그치다, 닦달하다, 질문을 퍼붓다

093
The decision's yours. Let me know tomorrow.
결정은 네 몫이야. 내일 알려줘.

The decision's yours 결정은 네 몫이야

094
The evidence you showed me, all that's no good. 증거를 내게 보여줬지만, 다 무용지물이야.

all that's no good 다 아무 소용도 없다

095
The exam start time has been pushed up a half an hour. 시험시작 시간이 30분 앞당겨졌어.

push the PT up a half an hour 발표회를 30분 당기다 push sth back to~ …을 늦추다

096
The hard part is still to come.
아직 힘든 상황은 오지 않았어.

097
The hard part is truly over.
힘든 상황은 정말 끝났어.

The hard part is~ 힘든 부분[상황]은 …이다 The easy part is~ 쉬운 부분은 …이다

098
The meal is ready. There you are.
음식이 준비됐어. 자 여기 있어.

There you are 물건주면서 여기 있어, 혹은 설명하면서 그것봐, 내가 뭐랬어, 그렇게 된거여어라는 의미.

099
The meeting was cancelled. End of story.
회의는 연기됐어. 그게 다야.

End of story 얘기 끝, 그게 다야

100
The next guy you see could turn out to be Mr. Right. 네가 보는 옆 사람이 너의 이상형이 될 수도 있어.

It turns out (that) S+V …로 판명나다 turn out to~…로 판명나다

101
The offer's still on the table?
그 제안 아직 유효한거지?

102
The point is, in a situation like this you got to pick sides.
이런 상황에서, 요점은 네가 어느 쪽이든 편을 들어야 된다는거야.

pick sides 편을 들다

103
The product never lived up to the hype.
이 제품은 화제를 모았던 만큼 기대를 충족시키지 못했어.

live up to the hype 사람들의 기대를 충족시키다, 화제된 것만큼 만족시키다

104
The same goes for you.
너도 마찬가지야.

105
The thing is I don't really believe you.
요는 내가 널 안 믿는다는거야.

The thing is~ 중요한 것은 …야

106
The thought never crossed my mind.
그 생각이 전혀 나질 않았어.

Sth cross one's mind …의 마음 속에 떠오르다 = come into one's mind

107
The trip has been cancelled. Go figure.
여행은 취소됐어. 확인해봐.

Go figure 확인해봐, 설명해봐

108
The video makes it clear you cheated.
이 동영상은 네가 바람피웠다는 것을 명백히 보여주고 있어.

make it clear …을 분명히 하다, 확실하게 하다

109
The weather is great, and I'm on the beach. What's not to like?
날씨는 끝내주고, 난 바닷가에 있는데 안좋을게 뭐 있어?

What's not to like? 정말 좋아(I like it)

110
The window closed on your hand? That had to hurt.
창문이 손등 위로 닫혔다고? 아팠겠다.

That had to hurt! 아팠겠다!

111
The worst part is I'm starting to get used to it.
최악은 내가 그거에 익숙해지고 있다는거야.

The worst part is~ 가장 최악은 …이다

112
Their alibi fell to pieces.
그들의 알리바이는 완전히 무너졌어.

fall to pieces 엉망이 되다, 무너지다

113

Then I quit, and you're screwed.

그럼 난 그만두고 넌 엿먹는거야.

be[get] screwed 엿먹다, 골탕먹다   screw sb 골탕먹이다

114

Then we're gonna take her out for a spin.

그리고 나서 우리는 배를 시험운행할거야.

take ~ out for a spin 시험운행하다

115

There are names for people like you now Bridge, you're a cougar, a MILF. 당신 같은 사람을 지칭하는 이름이 있어요, 브리짓. 당신은 젊은 남성을 노리는 중년여성이라구요.

116

There is a line, a line that should not be crossed. 넘어서는 안되는 선이 있어.

cross the line 선을 넘다   That's murder 너무하다, 불쾌하다

117

There it is.

뭔가 건네줄 때 자, 여기 있어.

118

There was something solid about her.

걔한테는 자기만의 색깔이 분명했어.

be solid about~ 믿음직스럽다, 성격이 좋다

119
There we are.
그래 맞아, 자, 됐다, 자, 다 왔다.

120
There were so many interesting things going on.
흥미로운 일들이 아주 많이 벌어지고 있었어.

~ sth going on 현재 벌어지고 있는 것

121
There will be hell to pay.
나중에 몹시 성가시게 될거야, 뒤탈이 생길텐데.

hell to pay 치루어야 할 대가, 뒤탈

122
There you go again.
또 시작이군, 그럼 그렇지.

123
There you go.
그래 그렇게 하는거야, 참 잘하는거야!, 그것 봐, 내 말이 맞지, 뭔가 건네주면서 자, 이거 받아, 여기 있어.

124
There you have it.
네 말이 옳아, 그렇게 된거야, 자 볼까, 자 됐어.

125
There's got to be a reason for that.
뭔가 그 이유가 있을거야.

There's got to be~ …가 있을거야

126
There's more to it than that.
다른 뭔가가 있어, 그것보다는 더 깊은 뜻이 있어.

127
There's no harm in looking for a girlfriend.
여친 구한다고 손해볼게 있나.

There's no harm in ~ing …해도 손해볼게 없어

128
There's no need to get upset.
화낼 필요가 없어.

get upset 화내다 go insane 미치다

129
There's no telling.
알 수가 없지, 모르지.

130
There's no way that that's a coincidence.
그게 우연의 일치일 리가 없어.

There's no way to+V[that S+V] …을 할 수가 없어, …할 방법이 없어, 절대 …일리가 없어

131
There's no way to talk him out of drinking.
걔 설득해서 술을 안마시게 할 방법이 없어.

talk sb out of~ 설득해서 …하지 못하게 하다

132
There's nobody home!
정신 어디다 두고 있는거야!

133
There's nothing you can do about it. So stop bitching.
그거 속수무책이야. 그러니까 더 이상 불평하지마.

(There's) Nothing you can do about it 너도 어쩔 수가 없어, 속수무책이야

134
There's nothing you can't do, if you put your mind to it.
네가 전념하면 못할 일은 없어.

put one's mind to~ 전념하다 = set one's mind to~

135
These days I'm all about you, baby.
요즘 난 너 뿐이야.

I'm all about sth[sth] …뿐이야, …가 정말 좋아

136
They all went unanswered.
그 편지들의 답장은 오지 않았어.

go unanswered 답장을 못받다

137

They are out of money? That would explain so much. 걔네들이 돈이 없다고? 말이 되네.

That would explain so much 말이 되다

138

They are too different. Their relationship can't go anywhere. 걔네들 너무 달라. 사귀는게 잘 될 수가 없어.

can't go anywhere 성공하지 못하다

139

They came out of nowhere and jumped me.

걔네들은 느닷없이 와서 내게 덤벼들었어.

out of nowhere 느닷없이, 난데없이

140

They decided to split up.

걔들은 헤어지기로 했어.

split up 헤어지다, 갈라서다

141

They decided to take a break from their relationship. 그들은 잠시 휴지기를 갖기로 했어.

take a break 연인들이 잠시 떨어지다

142

They gang up on me.

걔네들이 날 괴롭혀.

gang up on sb 집단으로 공격하다, 무리지어 괴롭히다

143

They got caught in the big rainstorm.
걔네들은 큰 폭풍우를 만났던거야.

get[be] caught in (곤란한 상황 등)에 처하다

144

They really hit it off.
정말 잘 통하더라고, 걔네들은 바로 좋아하더라고.

hit it off 만나자마자 죽이 잘 맞다, 통하다

145

They should be getting on with their careers.
걔네들은 경력을 계속 이어가야 해.

get on with~ 계속해서 …하다

146

They're always taking liberties, not giving much back in return.
걔네들은 항상 제멋대로 이용만 하고 보답하는 건 아무것도 없어.

take liberties with~ …을 함부로 대하다, 제멋대로 하다

147

They're even, so just leave it alone.
공평하니까 그냥 놔둬.

leave it alone 그거 그냥 놔두다

148

They're hanging around at the mall, as usual.
걔네는 언제나처럼 쇼핑몰에서 어슬렁거리고 있어.

as usual 여느 때처럼

149
They're outside cuddling on the balcony.
걔네들은 발코니에서 껴안고 있어.

cuddle 부둥켜안다

150
They've sacked me.
그들이 날 해고했어.

sack sb 자르다, 해고하다 = fire

151
Things are bad now, but things could be a lot worse. 지금 상황이 나쁘지만, 그나마 다행이야.

It could be worse 그나마 다행이야 It could be better 별로였어

152
Things are running a little bit late.
상황이 점점 늦어지고 있어.

be running late 늦다

153
Things will soon be back to normal.
상황이 곧 정상으로 돌아올거야.

be back to normal 정상으로 돌아가다

154
Thirty-one years old! Time flies, doesn't it?
31살이라고! 시간 정말 빨리 간다, 그지 않아?

How fast the time goes 시간이 어찌나 빨리 가던지

155
This can't be happening.
이건 있을 수가 없는 일이야, 이럴 수가.

156
This can't come as a total surprise to you.
이걸로 해서 넌 전혀 놀라지 않을거야.

come as a surprise 놀라다

157
This clock doesn't go with any of the stuff in my room.
이 시계는 내 방에 있는 물건들 중 어느 것하고도 어울리지 않아.

go with …와 어울리다, 조화되다

158
This girlfriend's got some serious issues with the relationship.
이 여친은 관계맺는데 심각한 문제가 있어.

I have ~issues with sb[sth] …한 문제가 있다

159
This is a special present. It's for you.
이거 아주 특별한 선물이야. 너 주려고.

It's for you 너 주려고

160
This is boring. What's all the fuss about?
지루하구만. 이게 다 무슨 소란이야?

What's all the fuss about? 이게 다 무슨 난리야?

161
This is by far the drunkest I've ever seen you.
여짓껏 네가 이렇게 취한 걸 본 적 없어.

by far 훨씬, 단연코

162
This is for you.
널 위해 준비했어, 이건 네 거야.

163
This is it. Take it or leave it.
이게 다야. 하든지 말든지.

This is it! 바로 이거야, 이게 다야! = That's it! 바로 그거야!, 이게 다야!

164
This is just me, like, being stupid.
바보같이 구는게 원래 나답죠.

That[It] is~ …답다, …가 그렇지 That[It] is not~ …답지 않아

165
This is just the thing to just perk you up.
이건 단지 너 기운나게 하려는거야.

perk sb up …을 기운나게 하다

166
This is my break and I'll take advantage of it.
나의 기회니까 내가 이용할거야.

This is my break 나의 기회야

167

This is not a rebound thing. I really got to love you. 땜빵용으로 사귀는거 아냐. 난 정말 널 사랑해.

be on the rebound 아직 실연중이다 **rebound thing** 실연 후 땜빵하고 사귀는 것

168

This is not my day.
정말 일진 안 좋네.

169

This is real gold. Guard it with your life.
이건 순금이야. 목숨걸고 지켜.

guard it with one's life 목숨걸고 그것을 지키다

170

This is so weird.
이건 정말 이상하다.

171

This is the only one that matters.
이것만이 유일하게 중요한 것이야.

~ that matters 중요한 것은 …야

172

This is what I'm talking about. What is up with you? 내가 하는 말은 바로 이거야. 너 무슨 문제있냐고?

What's up with~? …는 무슨 문제야?

173
This is where I draw the line.
여기까지가 내 한계야.

174
This isn't too revealing, is it?
너무 야하지 않지, 그지?

175
This job is about making the tough calls.
이 자리는 힘든 결정을 내리는 일이야.

be a tough call 결정하기 힘들다   make a tough call 힘든 결정을 하다

176
This morning my car broke down on the way to work. 오늘 아침에 출근 길에 차가 고장났어.

be on the way to~ …로 가는 중이야

177
This needs to be organized, not to mention cleaned up. 이건 청소는 말할 것도 없고 잘 정돈되어야 돼.

not to mention~ …은 말할 것도 없고

178
This one's for you.
이건 너를 위한거야.

179
This party rocks!
이 파티 끝내준다!

180
This seems difficult. What do you get out of this? 이거 어려워 보이는데. 이걸로 네가 얻는게 뭔데?

What do you get out of this? 이걸로 네가 얻는게 뭔데?

181
This time it's for real.
이번엔 진짜야.

for real 진짜야

182
This was some meet cute.
이건 운명적 만남이었어.

meet cute 운명적 첫 만남

183
This year all these things came more clearly to the fore. 금년에 이 모든 것들이 더욱 분명하게 표면화됐어.

come to the fore 표면화되다, 주목받다

184
Trust me, we got everything covered.
날 믿어, 우린 만반의 준비를 해놨어.

get everything covered 만반의 준비를 하다

185
Try to put a positive spin on it.
긍정적으로 바라보도록 해.

186
Turn yourself in to the police.
경찰에 자수해.

turn oneself in 자수하다

187
Twice I've let you slip through my fingers.
두번, 난 너를 놓쳤어.

let sb slip through one's fingers …을 놓치다

SCREEN TIPS

스크린에 자주 등장하는 형용사들

- **awful** 끔찍한, 지독한
- **bloody** 진짜 …해
- **fabulous** 믿어지지 않는, 굉장한, 멋진
- **pathetic** 한심한
- **huge** 굉장한
- **amazing** 놀라운
- **lousy** 형편없는, 야비한
- **weird** 이상야릇한, 기묘한
- **creepy** 오싹하는, 불쾌한
- **spooky** 으스스한
- **cute** 예쁘고 귀여운, 성적 매력이 있는
- **major** 주요한
- **gorgeous** 여자가 매력적인
- **naughty** 버릇없는, 야한
- **pushy** 뻔뻔한
- **cocky** 거만한, 우쭐한
- **revealing** 옷의 노출도가 심한

- **filthy** 더러운, 추잡한
- **groovy** 멋진, 근사한
- **fetching** 매력적인
- **curt** 퉁명스러운
- **kinky** 이상한, 변태스런
- **wacky** 괴짜의
- **chic** 멋진, 세련된
- **bossy** 으스대는
- **skanky** 몹시 불쾌한
- **hilarious** 아주 재미있는
- **disgusting** 역겨운
- **gross** 역겨운
- **chubby** 통통한
- **dodgy** 교활한
- **awkward** 서투른, 어설픈
- **slutty** 난잡한
- **awesome** 대단한, 멋진

188

Very funny!
(화난 어조로) 장난해!, 그래 우습기도 하겠다!, 말도 안돼!, 안 웃기거든!

189

Vicky was afraid of getting mugged.
비키는 노상강도를 당할까봐 무서웠어.

get[be] mugged 노상강도를 당하다

190

Wait a minute now, can I say something?
잠깐만, 뭐 좀 얘기할 수 있을까?

Can I say something? 뭐 좀 얘기할 수 있을까?

191

Wait a minute, let me get in on this.
잠깐, 나도 붙여줘.

be in on~ …에 연루되다 get sb in on~ …을 …에 함께 하게 해주다

192

Wait a minute. I got us coffee.
잠깐만. 내가 커피 사올게.

I got us coffee 내가 우리 커피 사[가져]올게

193

Wait. Don't hang up. Just listen to me.
기다려. 끊지마. 내 말 좀 들어봐.

hang up 전화를 끊다 a hang up call 받으면 끊어지는 전화

194

Want some more?
더 들래?, 더 먹을래?

195

Was it love at first sight?
그거 첫눈에 반한 사랑이었어?

love at first sight 첫눈에 반하다 unrequited love 짝사랑

196

Watch it. Watch your back.
조심해. 뒤를 조심하라고.

Watch it! 조심해!

197

Way to go son! I knew you'd find it!
잘했어, 아들아! 난 네가 그걸 발견할 줄 알았어!

Way to go! 잘한다 잘해!, 잘했다!

198

We also have a soft spot for the love.
우린 또한 사랑에 약해.

have a soft[weak] spot for~ …에 약하다, 사족을 못쓰다

199

We are going to make a killing tonight.
오늘 밤 떼돈 벌겠어.

make a killing 단기간에 떼돈을 벌다 = make a fortune

200

We can get laid anytime we want.
우린 원하면 언제라도 섹스를 할 수 있다는거야.

get laid 섹스하다

201

We can't leave her out in the cold.
걔를 제외시킬 수는 없어.

leave sb out in the cold …를 따돌리다

202

We could just snuggle or something.
그냥 껴안거나 뭐 그럴 수 있지.

snuggle 부둥켜안다

203

We don't need to put labels on it.
우리는 그거에 이름을 매길 필요는 없어.

put labels on~ 이름을 붙이다, 명명하다

204

We fell asleep. We were spooning.
우리 잠들었고 스푼모양으로 껴안고 있었어.

spoon 두개 스푼을 포개놓듯이 껴안다

205

We fixed the software. What else?
우리는 소프트웨어를 고쳤어. 다른 것은?

What else? 뭐 다른 것은?

206

We flogged our guts out to get this done.
우리는 이걸 마치기 위해 열심히 일했어.

flog one's guts out 열심히 일하다

207

We get our fair share of sightings.
우린 볼만큼 관광을 했어.

get one's fair share of~ 받아야 할 것을 받다

208

We go way back.
우리 알고 지낸 지 오래됐어, 우린 오랜 친구야.

go way back 서로 알고 지낸지 오래되었다

209

We got history.
우린 오랜 친분이 있잖아.

have[get] history 친분이 있다

210
We got off on the wrong foot.
시작이 좋지 못했던 것 같아.

get off on the wrong foot 시작이 잘못되다, 시작이 순조롭지 않다, 시작부터 어그러지다

211
We got on very well and sort of had relations.
우리는 사이좋게 지냈고 좀 사귀었어.

get on (well) with sb …와 사이가 좋다

212
We gotta get help.
도움을 받아야 해.

get help 도움을 받다

213
We had to find a place to lay low.
우린 숨어지낼 곳을 찾아야만 했어.

lay low 얌전히 있다, 잠수타다

214
We have to select a new member? Like who?
새로운 멤버를 뽑아야 한다고? 이를테면 누구?

Like who? 이를테면 누구처럼?

215
We hooked up, and we're been dating ever since.
우리는 관계를 시작해서 그 이후로 계속 데이트를 하고 있어.

hook up 만나다, 엮이다, 섹스하다

216

We just put ourselves out there, and what happened? 우리는 모든 걸 바쳤는데 어떻게 됐어?

put oneself out there 자신있게 나서다, 돕기 위해 무리한 노력을 하다

217

We just wanted to stop by and say good night.

잘자라고 말하려고 잠깐 들렀어.

say goodbye to~ 작별인사를 하다 say good night to~ 잘자라고 인사하다

218

We just wanted you to take a selfie of us.

네가 우리 셀카를 찍기를 바랬어.

take a selfie of~ 셀카를 찍다

219

We knocked him dead with our presentation.

우리는 발표회로 그를 감동시켰어.

knock sb dead 감동시키다, 놀라게 하다

220

We met once and we just clicked.

우리는 한번 만났는데 잘 어울렸어.

We just clicked 우린 바로 잘 어울렸어

221

We might as well be honest with each other.

우린 서로에게 솔직하는게 좋아.

might as well+V …하는게 나아

222
We need to fit it in before New York Fashion Week. 뉴욕 패션주간 전에 시간내서 해야 돼.

fit sth in 시간을 내서 …하다 fit sb in 시간을 내서 …보다

223
We need to get ourselves to the immigration office. 우리는 이민국에 출두해야 돼.

get oneself to+장소 …에 가다, …에 출두하다 get oneself+음식 내가 챙겨서 …을 먹다

224
We planned a birthday party. How about that?
생일파티를 준비했는데, 어때?

How about that? 이게 어때?, 이상하지?

225
We really have to be somewhere now.
이제 좀 다른데 가봐야 돼서.

have to be somewhere 다른 데 가봐야 돼

226
We should have never broken up. What was I thinking? 우리는 절대로 헤어지는게 아니었어. 내가 무슨 생각으로 그렇게 했을까?

What was I thinking? 내가 무슨 생각으로 그랬을까?

227
We signed a contract, so that's a lock.
우리는 계약서에 사인했으니 이제 분명해졌어.

That's a lock 분명하다, 확실하다

228
We thought you were a no show.
우리는 네가 안 오리라고 생각했어.

no show 약속을 해놓고 나타나지 않는 사람

229
We took shifts working on the project.
우리는 그 프로젝트 일을 돌아가면서 했어.

take shifts ~ing 돌아가면서 …하다

230
We walked away with the prize for the highest score. 우리는 최고 득점자상을 수상했어.

walk away with~ …을 타다, 얻다

231
We want to know how you got on.
우리는 네가 어떻게 잘 해냈는지 알고 싶어.

~ how you got on 어떻게 잘 해냈는지

232
We went to high school together.
우리는 고등학교 동창이야.

went to college together 동창이다

233
We were a square peg and a round hole.
우리는 서로 어울리지 않았어.

be a square peg and round hole 잘 어울리지 않다

234
We were out of our minds in love.
우리는 사랑 때문에 제정신이 아니었어.

be[go] out of one's mind 제정신이 아니다, 미치다

235
We were worried sick about you.
우리는 너 때문에 걱정이 태산이었어.

I'm worried (sick) about~ …가 무척 걱정이야

236
We will make time to hang out with each other. 서로 함께 있을 시간을 내보자.

make time to+V/for+N …할 시간을 내다

237
We'll be rubbing shoulders with rockstars.
우리는 락스타들과 어울릴거야.

rub shoulders with~ …와 어울리다

238
We'll be together, no matter what the future holds. 미래가 어떻게 될지 몰라도 우리는 함께 할거야.

No matter what the future holds 미래가 어떻게 될지 몰라

239
We'll get back to you as soon as we can.
가능한 한 빨리 전화드릴게요.

get back to sb (on sth) (…건으로) …에게 나중에 전화를 다시 하다

240
We'll have to push the reservation to another night. 우리 예약을 다른 저녁으로 미뤄야 될 것 같아요.

push the reservation 예약을 미루다

241
We'll sort it out.
우리는 그것을 해결할거야.

sort ~ out …을 해결하다

242
We'll throw Mike a send-off party just before he leaves. 우리는 마이크가 떠나기 전에 송별회를 해줄거야.

throw sb a send-off party 송별회를 열다

243
We're almost there.
거의 다 됐어, 거의 끝났어.

244
We're almost there. Be patient now.
거의 다 왔어. 조금만 참아.

be almost there 거의 목표에 다다르다

245
We're behind you a hundred percent.
우리는 100% 너를 지지해.

be behind sb …의 편이다, 지지하다

246
We're booked solid for the next month!
다음 달엔 예약이 꽉 차 있다구!

be booked solid 모두 예약되다

247
We're clear on that?
우리 그 점에 있어서는 확실한거죠?

be[get] clear on …에 대해 확실히 하다   to be clear 분명히 하자면

248
We're done for the day.
그만 가자, 그만 하자.

249
We're done here.
우린 얘기 끝났어.

250
We're friends. Level with me.
우린 친구야. 내게 솔직히 말해.

level with sb 솔직히 털어놓다 = be on the level with sb

251
We're going to have sex? Get a condom!
우리 섹스할거지? 콘돔 가져와!

Get a condom! 콘돔을 챙겨!

252
We're gonna straighten things out.
우리는 상황을 제대로 바로 잡을거야.

straighten it out 일을 제대로 바로 잡다

253
We're having a going-away party for Susan.
수잔을 위해 송별파티를 할거야.

have a going-away party for sb …을 위해 송별파티를 하다

254
We're having second thoughts about it.
다시 생각해봐야겠어.

255
We're heading to a club. Are you in?
우리 클럽에 가는 길인데, 너도 갈래?

Are you in? 너도 할래?

256
We're heading to Las Vegas to get hitched.
우리는 결혼하기 위해 라스베거스로 갈거야.

get hitched 결혼하다

257
We're just going through a little bit of a rough patch. **우리는 좀 힘든 시기를 겪고 있어.**

go through sth …을 겪다, 경험하다 rough patch 어려운 시기, 힘든 시기

258
We're just goofing around.
그냥 빈둥거리고 있는거야.

goof off 농땡이 치다 goof around 빈둥거리며 시간을 보내다

259
We're not gonna make a bigger deal out of this than it already is.
실제 이상으로 큰 일이 난 것처럼 소동피지말자.

make a big deal out of~ 과장하다, …으로 큰 소동을 부리다

260
We're not moving, end of discussion.
우린 이사가지 않을거야, 더 이상 토론은 없어.

End of discussion 더 이상 말마

261
We're not under any illusions that you two don't sleep in the same bed.
너희 둘이 같은 침대에서 안잔다는 것을 우리는 정확히 알고 있어.

be not under any illusions that ~ …에 속지 않다, 상황을 정확히 알다

262
We're on a break. I don't know if we'll get back together.
잠시 냉각중인데 다시 사귈지 모르겠어.

be on a break 연인들이 잠시 떨어져지내다

263
We're planning to go grab a bite to eat.
우리는 좀 간단히 요기를 채울 생각이야.

grab[take, have] a bite (to eat) 간단히 요기하다

264
We're pulling out all the stops.
최선을 다하고 있어요.

pull out all the stops 최선을 다하다 make the best of~ 최선을 다하다

265
We're taking some time apart;
우리는 당분간 떨어져 지내고 있어;

take[spend] some time apart 당분간 떨어져 지내다

266
We've been stuck on this for an hour.
한 시간동안 이거에 막혀 있어.

be stuck on~ …에 막혀 있다, …에 미치다

267
We've fucked up utterly.
우리 완전히 망쳤어.

fuck sb[sth] up은 「…의 신세나 상황을 망치다」라는 뜻으로 그냥 목적어없이 fuck up처럼 쓰이기도 한다.

268
We've got to finish. That's the thing!
우리는 일을 끝내야 해. 바로 그거야!

That's the thing! 바로 그거지! = That's the spirit!

269
We've gotta get something to eat.
우린 뭘 좀 먹어야겠어.

270
Well done. It tasted great.
잘했어. 아주 맛이 좋아.

Well done! 잘했어! Very well done! 아주 잘했어!

271
Well, tell him to fuck off.
저기, 걔보고 꺼져달라고 해.

fuck off는 아주 무례한 go away. 상대방보고 「그만 꺼져라」라고 말하는 표현이다. Fuck off out of here! 라고 할 수도 있다.

272
Well, that puts us back at square one.
저기, 그렇게 되면 원점이네.

be back to the square one 원점으로 돌아가다

273
Whaddaya mean, you didn't take it?
무슨 말야, 네가 거절했다고?

274
What a beautiful dress. You're a vision.
드레스 멋지다. 정말 눈부셔.

You're a vision 눈이 부시다, 좋아 보여 You are something else 넌 특별해

275
What a funny joke. That's a classic!
참 재미있는 농담이네. 정말 재미있어!

That's a classic 전형적이야

276
What a great job! Attaboy!
참 멋지게 했어! 잘했어!

Attaboy! 잘했어! Attagirl! 잘했어!

277
What a letdown!
참 실망이다!

letdown 실망, 낙담

278
What a nice surprise. Would you like to come in? 이게 누구야. 들어와라.

What a (nice) surprise! 이게 누구야!

279
What a relief!
아, 다행이야!

280
What am I doing with my life?
내가 인생을 어떻게 살아가고 있는거지?

What am I doing with you? 내가 지금 너하고 뭐하는거지?

> 281

What are the odds?
가능성은 어때?, 확률이 얼마야?

> 282

What are we doing staying together?
우리 함께 있으면서 뭐하는거지?

What are we doing? 우리 무슨 관계야?

> 283

What are you all dressed up for?
웬일로 그렇게 쫙 빼입은거야?

be all dressed up 옷을 멋지게 차려 입다

> 284

What are you doing? Are you leaving? Wait.
뭐하는거야? 가는거야? 기다려.

I'm leaving 나 간다. leave란 동사는 「(나)가다」라는 단순한 의미이지만, 모임에 있다가 그만 나갈 때도, 다른 지역으로 좀 멀리 간다고 할 때도 쓰인다.

> 285

What are you talking about? When did this happen? 무슨 소리야? 언제 이랬는데?

What are you talking about? 무슨 얘기를 하는거야?, 그게 무슨 말이야?

> 286

What are you up to this Christmas Eve?
크리스마스 이브에 뭐 할거야?

be up to sth …을 꾸미고 있다, …할 수 있다

287

What are you waiting for?
기다릴게 뭐 있어.

288

What brought that on?
어떻게 그렇게 된거야?

bring sth on 초래하다, 야기하다

289

What brought you up there?
뭐 때문에 거기에 온거야?

What brings[brought]~? 왜 …에 온거야?

290

What can I say? I like her.
뭐랄까? 난 걔가 좋아.

What can I say? 할 말이 없네, 뭐랄까?, 나더러 어쩌라는거야?

291

What do I do with that?
그걸 어떻게 하지?

What do I do with~? …을 어떻게 하지?

292

What do you do in your spare time?
여유시간에는 뭐해?

What do you do? 지금 뭐해?

293
What do you know?
1. (비아냥) …에 대해 네가 뭘 알아? 2. (놀람) 정말

294
What do you mean by that? Am I fat?
그게 무슨 말이야? 내가 뚱뚱하다고?

What do you mean? 그게 무슨 말이야? = What do you mean by that?

295
What do you mean you got fired?
잘렸다니 그게 무슨 말이야?

What do you mean S+V? …가 무슨 말이야?

296
What do you mean, too late?
너무 늦었다니 그게 무슨 말이야?

What do you mean, ~? …가 무슨 말이야?

297
What do you say to meeting some of my friends?
내 친구들 좀 만나는게 어때?

What do you say to+명사[~ing]? …하는게 어때?

298
What do you say we get together for a drink?
만나서 술 한잔하면 어때?

What do you say S+V? …하는게 어때?

299
What do you say?
(상대방의 동의를 구하며) 어때?, 네 생각은?

300
What do you see in her? I don't understand it.
걔 뭐가 좋은거야? 난 이해가 안돼.

see in sb …을 좋아하다

301
What do you take me for?
날 뭘로 보는거야?

take A for B A를 B로 생각하다, 잘못 알다

302
What do you think about me staying the night?
내가 남아서 밤을 보내는거 어떻게 생각해?

What do you think of[about]~? …을 어떻게 생각해?

303
What do you think it will be like?
그게 어떨 것 같아?

304
What do you think? Should we show them the room?
네 생각은 어때? 걔네한테 방을 보여줘야 돼?

What do you think (of that)? 네 생각은 어때?

305
What do you want from me?
내게 뭘 원하는거야?, 나보고 어쩌라는거야?

306
What do you want to do with your life?
네 삶을 어떻게 살아가고 싶어요?

What do you want to do with~? …을 어떻게 하고 싶어?

307
What does that prove?
그래서?, 그래서 그게 어쨌다는거야?

308
What does that tell us?
이게 무슨 말이겠어?

309
What does your heart tell you? Yes or no?
솔직히 말해봐. 예스야 노야?

What does your heart tell you? 네 마음은 뭐라고 하는데?, 솔직하게 말해봐

310
What else is new?
뭐 더 새로운 소식은 없어?, 그게 다야?

311

What for? I didn't do anything wrong.
뭐 때문에? 난 아무런 잘못을 한 게 없는데.

What for? 뭐 때문에?

312

What happened with you and Peter?
피터랑 무슨 일 있었어?

What happened (to you)? 무슨 일이야?, 어떻게 된거야?

313

What has come over you?
왜 그런거야?

314

What have you done with my girlfriend?
내 여친을 어떻게 했니?

What have you done with~ ? …을 어떻게 한거야?, …에게 무슨 짓을 한거야?

315

What in the hell do you think you're doing?
너 이게 도대체 무슨 짓이야?

What do you think you're doing? 이게 무슨 짓이야?, 너 정신나갔어?

316

What is that supposed to mean?
그게 무슨 의미인거야?

Sth be supposed to+V …하기로 되어 있다

317
What is this fuss about?
왜들 이 난리야?
fuss 야단법석, 호들갑

318
What makes you think so?
왜 그렇게 생각해?

319
What makes you think you're right?
어째서 네가 옳다고 생각하는거야?
What makes you think S+V? 왜 그렇게 생각해?

320
What the heck? Do it anyway.
어쩌라고? 어쨌든 하라고.
What the hell[heck]! 도대체 뭐야? 에라 모르겠다!

321
What the hell are you doing here?
도대체 여기서 뭐하니?
What the hell[heck] are you doing here? 도대체 여긴 어쩐 일이야?

322
What the hell is wrong with you?
도대체 무슨 일이야?, 뭐 잘못됐어?
be wrong with …가 잘못되거나 틀리다

323

What took you so long? I called you hours ago.
왜 이리 늦었어? 몇 시간 전에 전화했어.

What took you so long? 왜 이리 늦은거야?　I won't be long 금방 올게(I'll be back in a tick)

324

What took you so long?
왜 이렇게 오래 걸렸어?, 왜 이렇게 늦었어?

325

What was I thinking?
내가 왜 그랬을까?

326

What would happen if I went on a diet?
내가 다이어트를 하면 어떻게 될까?

I've been on a diet 다이어트 하는 중이다

327

What would I have done without you?
네가 없었더라면 어쩔 뻔했어?

328

What would you say?
어떻게 할거야?, 넌 뭐라고 할래?

329
What, like, are we going steady?
뭐 우리 사귀기라도 하는거야?

go steady 사귀다 go steady는 「…와 지속적으로 교제하다」라는 뜻.

330
What'd I tell you?
그러게 내가 뭐랬어?

331
What're the symptoms?
증상이 어때요?

332
What're you doing here? You can't be here!
여기서 뭐해? 여기 있으면 안 돼!

What are you doing here? 여긴 어쩐 일이야?, 여기서 뭐하는거야?

333
What're you doing? You scared me half to death. 뭐해? 정말 놀랬잖아.

You scared me! 놀랬잖아! **Don't be scared** 놀래지마 **half to death** 죽도록, 너무나

334
What's done is done
이미 끝난 일이야, 이미 엎질러진 물인데

335
What's goin' on?
무슨 일이야?

336
What's going on with you, buddy?
어이 친구, 너 무슨 일이야?

What's going on with sb? …는 무슨 일이야?

337
What's got into you?
뭣 때문에 이러는거야?

338
What's it got to do with us?
그게 우리와 무슨 상관이야?

have (got) to do with~ …와 관련이 있다, …에 관한 것이다

339
What's it like? I've never been there.
어떤대? 가본 적이 없어서.

What's it like? 그거 어때?

340
What's it to you?
그게 너랑 무슨 상관이지?

341
What's the big deal?
별거 아냐?, 무슨 큰 일이라도 있는거야?

342
What's the catch?
속셈이 뭐야?, 무슨 꿍꿍이야?, 조건이 뭔데?

343
What's the harm in believing?
믿어서 손해볼 것 있어?

No harm done 괜찮아

344
What's the harm?
손해볼게 뭐야?, 밑질거 없어

345
What's the matter with you? What is your problem? 무슨 일이야? 무슨 문제야?

What's the[your] problem? 문제가 뭐야?

346
What's the matter with you?
무슨 일이야?, 도대체 왜 그래?

347
What's the story with you two, anyway?
그나저나, 너희 둘은 어떻게 되는거야?

What's the story? 상황은 어때?

348
What's the worst(thing) that could happen?
무슨 나쁜 일이야 생기겠어?

349
What's there to know?
뻔한거 아냐?

350
What's with you?
뭐 땜에 그래?

351
What's wrong? What have I done?
뭐가 잘못됐어? 내가 어쨌는데?

What have I done? 내가 어쨌는데?, 내가 무슨 짓을 한거지?

352
What's your take on this?
넌 이것에 대해 어떻게 생각해?

What's your take on~ ? …에 대해 어떻게 생각해? have a fresher take on~ 신선한 견해를 갖다

353

Whatever I said, I was drunk, I didn't mean it.
내가 뭐라 했든, 난 취했었어. 일부러 그런게 아냐.

I didn't mean it[that] 일부러 그런 것은 아냐

354

Whatever you got going on, fill me in.
무슨 일이든, 내게 알려줘.

fill sb in …에게 상세한 정보를 알려주다 = catch sb up

355

When all is said and done, you must tell the truth.
모든 걸 고려해볼 때, 넌 진실을 말해야 돼.

when all is said and done 모든 것을 고려해볼 때

356

When did you pick up on that?
언제 알아차렸어?

357

When do you think you fell in love with your wife?
부인하고는 언제부터 사랑에 빠지게 된 것 같아요?

fall in love with …와 사랑에 빠지다

358

When I was young, I didn't have two dimes to rub together.
어릴 적에는 빈털터리었어.

not have two dimes to rub together 빈털터리이다

359
When is this[it] due?
이게 언제 마감이야?

be due 마감이다

360
When is your baby due?
출산예정이 언제야?

When is the baby due? 출산예정일이 언제야? the baby 대신 it을 써도 된다.

361
When would you be available to start the job?
언제 출근할 수 있으세요?

be available to~ …가 가능하다

362
Where am I supposed to put all my stuff?
내 물건 다 어디에다 놓아야 돼?

be supposed to~ …하기로 되어 있다, …해야 한다

363
Where are we? Where is this relationship going?
우린 어떤 관계야? 이 관계가 어떻게 되어가는거야?

Where are we? 여기가 어디야?, 우리 무슨 관계야?

364
Where are you going with this, Chris?
크리스, 무슨 말을 하려는거야?

I don't know where this is going 어떻게 돌아가는지 모르겠어

365
Where are your manners?
왜 이렇게 버릇이 없어?

366
Where can I reach him?
걔 연락처가 어떻게 되나요?

reach sb …와 통화하다 on hold 전화중 기다리고 있는

367
Where did we leave off?
어디까지 했더라?

Where was I? 어디까지 했더라? = Where were we? = Where did we leave off?

368
Where does it say that?
무슨 근거로 그렇게 말하는거야?, 어디에 그렇게 씌여 있어?

Where does it say that S+V? 무슨 근거로 …라고 말하는거야?

369
Where does that leave us?
그럼 우린 어떻게 되는거야?

lose one's mind(= lose it) 정신나가다, 제 정신이 아니다

370
Where is my car? Is this some kind of joke?
내 차 어디에 있어? 이거 뭐 장난치는거야?

Is this some kind of joke? 농담한거지?

371

Where was he last seen?
걔를 마지막으로 본게 어디야?

be last seen 마지막으로 목격되다

372

Where're your manners? Aren't you gonna invite us in? 예의를 지켜라. 우리 안으로 초대안할거야?

Where're your manners? 예의를 갖춰라 = Mind manners!

373

Who are you to say something like that?
네가 뭔데 그런 말을 하는거야?

something like that 뭐 그런 비슷한 것

374

Who cares? I didn't like her anyway.
알게 뭐람? 난 어쨌거나, 걔 싫어.

Who cares? 신경안써, 상관없어

375

Who could[would] have thought?
누가 생각이나 했겠어?, 상상도 못했네.

376

Who do you think you're talking to?
왜 소리를 지르는거야? 날 바보로 아는거야?

Who do you think you're talking to? 날 바보로 아는거야?

377
Who knows what could happen?
무슨 일이 일어날지 아무도 몰라.

Who knows ~? …을 누가 알겠어?

378
Who said anything about talking?
누가 얘기만 한대?

379
Who says I can't handle it?
누가 내가 그걸 처리할 수 없을거라고 말하는거야?

Who says you failed? 네가 실패했다고 누가 그래?

380
Who's to say it wasn't you?
네가 아니라는 걸 누가 알 수 있겠어?

Who can say S+V? 누가 알 수 있겠어? = Who's to say S+V?

381
Why (do you) put me through this?
왜 이렇게 힘들게 하는거야?

382
Why are you still miffed at me?
넌 왜 아직도 나한테 화나있는거야?

be miffed at sb[about sth] 화를 내다

383
Why can't you ever take my side?
넌 왜 내 편을 들어줄 수 없는거야?

take one's side …의 편을 들다 = take sides

384
Why didn't you answer your cell phone?
왜 핸드폰 안 받았어?

385
Why didn't you return any of my calls?
왜 내 전화에 한번도 전화를 해주지 않은거야?

return one's call …에게 콜백(답신) 전화를 하다

386
Why do you look so unhappy? Cheer up.
왜 그리 안 좋아 보여? 힘내.

Cheer up! 힘내!, 기운내!

387
Why does it come to this?
어쩌다 이 지경에 이르렀어?

come to this 이 지경에 이르다, 이런 상황이 되다

388
Why don't you just leave me alone?
그냥 나 좀 놔둬?

leave sb alone …을 가만히 두다

389
Why don't you take it easy on your girlfriend?
네 여친에게 심하게 하지마.

take it easy on~ 천천히 하다, 심하게 하지 않다

390
Why don't you, like, ever realize the truth?
너, 뭐랄까, 현실을 깨달아야 하지 않겠니?

391
Why haven't you ever told me about it?
왜 여태까지 그것에 대해 내게 말하지 않은거야?

392
Why is it that you're not coming?
넌 왜 안오는거야?

You're not coming? 너 안올거야?

393
Why is it you aren't quite yourself at the moment?
넌 지금 왜 이렇게 제 정신이 아닌거야?

be oneself~ …다워, 제정신이다

394
Why not ask her about it?
걔한테 그거 물어보는 게 어때?

Why not+N? …는 왜 안되는거야? Why not+V? …하는게 어때?

395
Why not? Is there something up?
왜 안돼? 무슨 일 생겼어?

Something's up 일이 좀 생겼어(Something is up)

396
Why not? It's a good chance.
왜 안돼? 좋은 기회인데.

Why not? 왜 안돼?, 그러지 뭐

397
Why rock the boat, is what I'm thinking.
내 생각은 왜 평지풍파를 일으키냐는거야.

rock the boat 평지풍파를 일으키다

398
Why would I lie to someone I'm fairly fond of?
내가 그렇게 좋아하는 사람에게 왜 거짓말을 하겠어?

be fond of~ …을 좋아하다

399
Why would you say that?
왜 그런 소리를 해?, 무슨 이유로 그런 말을 해?

400
Will do. I'll call you on your cell phone.
좋아. 네 핸드폰으로 전화할게.

Will do 알았어, 그렇게 = I will do that

401
Will you go get her, Andy?
앤디야, 가서 걔를 데려와라.

go get her 그녀를 데려와, 가서 그녀를 잡다. Go get her처럼 단수로 쓰이면, 단순히 "…을 데려와라," " 잡아와라"라는 뜻.

402
Will you go out with me on New Year's Eve?
신년제야에 함께 데이트할래요?

403
Will you go out with me?
나랑 사귈래?

go out with sb 사귀다

404
Will you sleep over with me tonight?
오늘밤 나랑 같이 자고 놀래?

sleep over 하룻밤 놀고 먹고 자다

405
Will you stop? This is nuts.
그만 좀 할래? 이건 미친 짓이야.

go[be] nuts 미치다, 무척 화내다 drive sb nuts[crazy] 돌게 만들다

406
Wish me luck.
행운을 빌어줘.

407

With all due respect.
(반대의견을 말하면서 공손함을 표시) 그렇긴 한데요.

408

Word travels fast.
발없는 말이 천리 가, 소문은 빨리 돌잖아.

409

Work didn't help on that score either.
직장도 그 점에 있어서는 도움이 되지 않았다.

on that score 그 점에 있어서는

410

Would it be better if it was all for nothing?
다 수포로 돌아가면 더 낫겠어?

be all for nothing 수포로 돌아가다

411

Would you get a load of him?
저 사람을 좀 봐봐?

get a load of~ …을 보다

412

Would you keep an eye on this for me?
이거 좀 봐줄래요?

have (get) one's eye on~ 눈독들이다 have[keep] an eye on 주의깊게 지켜보다

413

Would you like me to get out of here?
내가 여기서 나갈까?

Get out of here!라고 하면 소리치면서 꼴도 보기 싫으니까 "여기서 당장 나가라," "꺼져라(Go away!)," 혹은 문맥에 따라 말도 안되는 소리하지 말라는 뜻이 된다.

414

Would you like to walk me to my car?
내 차 있는데까지 함께 걸어가 줄테야?

walk sb to the car 차 있는데까지 …와 함께 걸어가다

SCREEN TIPS

스크린에서나 볼 수 있는 단어들.

- **thing :** 어떤 것을 대강 뭉뚱그려서 말할 때 쓸 수 있는 편리한 단어가 바로 thing이다. 스크린을 보다보면 job thing, party thing 같은 말이 많이 들리는데 이는 이미 앞에서 언급하였거나 혹은 다시 이야기 안해도 서로 알고 있는 상황을 얼버무려 지칭하는 말.

- **~, though :** 문장 중간에 혹은 할 말 다 해놓고 문장 끝에다 though를 살짝 덧붙이는 걸 자주 들을 수 있다. 이렇게 문장 끝에 붙은 though는 「그래도」, 「그러나」의 의미.

- **like :** 우리말에서도 "에~, 그~, 뭐랄까~"등을 특별한 의미없이 문장 중간 중간에 삽입하듯이, like는 특히 젊은 사람들이 별다른 의미없이 말하는 중간 중간에 사용하는 단어이다. 종종 강조하고 싶은 말 앞에 의도적으로 집어넣기도 한다.

- **creep :** creep이 동사로 「…를 거북하게 하다, 징그럽게 만들다」라는 뜻의 creep sb out의 형태로 자주 사용된다. 명사로는 「아니꼬운 사람, 재수없는 사람」을 지칭하며 또 복수형으로 써서 「섬뜩한 느낌」을 뜻하기도 한다. 「비굴한」, 「아니꼬운」, 「재수없는」이라는 뜻의 형용사형 creepy도 흔히 들을 수 있는 단어.

- **phase :** 「단계, 국면」하면 얼핏 stage라는 단어가 떠오른다. 그러나 구어에서는 phase라는 단어를 즐겨 쓰는데, 일련의 과정 속 「단계」 및 「행동 양식」을 의미한다.

- **~ person :** 간단히 「…을 좋아하는 사람」 혹은 「…스타일의 사람」을 지칭할 때 ~ person이라는 말을 많이 쓴다. 아침형 인간은 morning person, 강아지를 좋아하는 사람은 dog person이라고 한다.

- **could use :** 「…가 필요하다」, 「…이 있으면 좋겠다」

415

Yeah, maybe so, but a deal's a deal. I'm sorry.
그래, 아마도 그렇지. 다만 약속은 약속이잖아, 미안해.

That's not the deal 얘기가 다르잖아 A deal's a deal 약속은 약속이야

416

You (have) got the wrong idea.
잘못 짚었네.

417

You accepted my apology. We're all good?
내 사과를 받아들였으니 우리 문제 없는거지?

We're all good? 우리 문제없는거지?

418

You act like this is a disaster.
큰 일 난 것처럼 행동하네.

It's a disaster 끔찍한 일이야, 엉망이야

419
You already hit on me an hour ago.
한 시간 전에 이미 유혹했는데요.

hit on sb 유혹하다, 꼬시다

420
You always get your way.
넌 항상 네 멋대로 해.

get one's way …가 하고 싶은대로 하다, …멋대로 하다

421
You always say that you're smarter than everyone else. 넌 항상 네가 다른 사람보다 더 똑똑하다고 그러더라.

You always say that 넌 항상 그렇게 말하더라

422
You are always angry. Where does it come from? 넌 항상 화를 내. 왜 그러는거야?

Where does[did] it come from? 어디서 난거야?, 왜 그러는거야? 이는 이해할 수 없는 상대방의 언행에 "왜 그러는거야?"라고 물어보는 문장.

423
You are in the wrong on this.
이건 네가 잘못했어.

be in the wrong (about/on)~ (…에 대해) 잘못하다

424
You are not to see him anymore.
넌 더 이상 걔를 만나지 마라.

see sb …와 사귀다, 만나다

425
You are not yourself.
제정신이 아니네.

426
You are really not a morning person.
넌 아침형 인간이 절대 아니구나.

427
You are right on the money.
바로 맞혔어, 바로 그거야, 맞는 말이야.

428
You are right. I'll give you that one.
네 말이 맞아. 그건 그래.

I'll give you that one 네 말이 맞아, 그건 그래

429
You are scored on my heart.
당신은 내 맘에 새겨져 있어요.

be scored on one's heart …의 마음에 새겨져 있다

430
You are too noisy. Cut it out.
너 너무 시끄러워. 그만둬.

Cut it out! 그만둬!

431

You asked for it.
자업자득이지, 네가 자초한 일이잖아, 그런 일을 당해도 싸다.

432

You asked her to leave? That's it?
걔보고 떠나라고 했어? 그걸로 끝이야?

That's it! 그게 다야!, 이게 끝이야!, 바로 그거야! = That's that

433

You bastard! You ruined my life!
나쁜 놈! 네가 내 인생을 망쳤어!

434

You bend over backwards.
넌 최선을 다해, 안간힘을 다 쓰고 있어.

bend over backwards 최선을 다해 …하려고 하다, 안간힘을 다 쓰다

435

You bet. I wouldn't miss it.
물론이지. 꼭 갈게.

You bet 물론이지, 그럼, 확실해　I'll bet 틀림없어

436

You better believe it. This is happening.
정말이야. 정말 그렇다니까.

This is happening 이렇게 되다니

437
You can count on me.
나한테 말겨, 날 믿어도 좋아.

438
You can crash in my bedroom.
내 침실에서 자도 돼.
crash in one's bed(room) …의 침대에서 자다

439
You can go leave work and go home now.
퇴근하고 집에 가도 좋아.
I'm leaving 나 그만둔다 leave work 퇴근하다, 퇴사하다

440
You can leave us, thanks Tony.
자리 좀 비켜줘, 고마워 토니.
You can leave us 자리를 좀 비켜주라, 가도 돼 steal sb away 데리고 가다

441
You can say that again.
그렇고 말고, 정말 그래, 동감이야.

442
You can still make it work, right?
넌 아직 잘 돌아가게 할 수 있지, 맞지?
make it[this] happen 잘 돌아가게 하다

443
You can't be serious.
정말이야, 말도 안돼, 그럴 리가, 장난하는거지?

444
You can't die on me.(=Don't die on me)
죽지마.

445
You can't do that!
그러면 안되지!

446
You can't do this to me.
내게 이러면 안되지.

447
You can't go wrong with this.
이건 잘못되는 법이 없어.

448
You cannot keep going like this.
너 이렇게 계속할 수는 없지.

keep ~ing 계속해서 …하다

449

You caught me doing it with Chris. What's the big deal? 내가 크리스와 그거하는거 너한테 들켰는데 그게 뭐 대수야?

do it (with sb) (…와) 섹스하다

450

You caught me. I am so busted.
들켰네. 딱 걸렸어.

I'm so busted 딱 걸렸네 I'm caught 딱 걸렸어

451

You cheated on me after I cheated on you. Touche. 내가 바람폈다고 네가 맞바람을 펴. 내가 졌다.

Touche 내가 졌어, 인정할게

452

You decide.
네가 결정해.

453

You deserve it. You're a good writer.
넌 그럴 자격이 돼. 넌 정말 좋은 작가야.

You deserve it 넌 그래도 돼 You more than deserve it 충분히 그러고도 남아

454

You deserve to be happy. And so do I.
넌 행복할 자격이 돼. 나도 그렇고.

So does Chris 크리스도 그래 So do I 나도 그래 Me neither 나도 안그래

455
You did a good job! I was very impressed.
정말 잘 했어! 매우 인상적이었어.

You did a good job 잘했어

456
You did what? I can't believe it.
뭘했다고? 안 믿어져.

You did what? 뭘 어쨌다고? You're what? 뭘 어쩐다고?

457
You did? What was he talking about?
그랬어? 걔는 뭐랬어?

You did? 그랬어? You do? 그래?

458
You didn't have to walk me all the way back up here. 여기까지 나를 다시 바래다줄 필요는 없었어.

459
You didn't let me down. You did the right thing. 넌 날 실망시키지 않았어. 제대로 했어.

You did the right thing 올바른 일을 했어

460
You do that.
그렇게 해.

461
You do the math.
잘 생각해봐, 계산해봐.

462
You don't belong here.
여기에 오면 안돼.

463
You don't get it. She and I are no longer friends.
모르는구만. 걔하고 난 더 이상 친구아냐.

You don't get it 넌 아직 이해못해, 뭘 모르는구만 I don't get it 이해가 안돼

464
You don't have a care in the world?
걱정거리가 하나도 없어?

care 근심, 신경쓰다

465
You don't know the first thing about it.
쥐뿔도 모르면서.

466
You don't let that slip through your fingers.
그걸 떨어뜨리지마.

let sth slip through one's fingers …을 놓치다

467
You don't mean it. You're just angry.
진심 아니지. 넌 그냥 화가 난거야.

You don't mean it[that] 장난이지

468
You don't mean that.
너 정말 아니지.

469
You don't say!
1. (가벼운 놀람, 불확실) 설마!, 그럴리가!, 정말? 2. (다 아는얘기) 뻔한 거 아냐?

470
You don't want to freak her out.
걔를 놀라게 하지마라.

sb[sth] freak sb out 놀라게 하다, 질겁하게 하다

471
You dumped her right before her birthday?
걔 생일 바로 전에 걔를 차버렸니?

dump sb 차버리다 = ditch, get ditched = get dumped 차이다

472
You get to fool around with a totally hot chick.
넌 섹시한 핫걸과 놀아나고 있구나.

fool around 빈둥거리다, 바람피다

473

You get what you pay for.
땀을 흘린 만큼 얻는거야, 지불한 만큼 받아.

474

You go back out there and try harder.
다시 더 열심히 뛰어야지.

get[go] back out there 다시 뛰다 = get back on one's feet

475

You got a gut feeling on this?
이거에 본능적으로 오는 느낌이 있어?

get[have] a gut feeling 어떤 직감을 느끼다

476

You got it. Now keep on going.
맞아. 이제 계속 하라고.

You got it 알았어, 맞아, 바로 그거야 You got it[that]? 알아들었어?, 알겠어?

477

You got me there, but you're wrong about this!
그건 네가 맞아, 하지만 이건 네가 틀렸어!

You got me there 모르겠어, 네 말이 맞아

478

You got me. What do you want?
내가 졌어. 원하는게 뭐야?

You got me 너한테 졌다, 나 몰라, 알아차렸네, 들켰네

479

You got so much about you that will make you successful. 너는 성공할 가능성이 아주 높아.

You got so much about you 전도가 유망하다

480

You got the day off? Well played!
하루 휴가를 받았어? 잘했어!

Well played! 잘했어!

481

You got[have] a point there.
네 말이 맞아, 네 말에 일리가 있어.

482

You gotta do what you gotta do.
할 일은 해야지.

483

You gotta man up and just go for it.
넌 남자답게 그냥 한번 해봐야지.

man up 남자답게 행동하다

484

You had a beef with him.
넌 걔한테 불만이 있어, 넌 걔랑 다퉜어.

have a beef with sb …에 불만이 있다, 문제가 있다

485

You had it coming. You refused to study.

네가 자초한거야. 공부하기 싫어했잖아.

have sth coming 어려운 상황을 자초하다

486

You have 30 seconds to pull your shit together, OK? 30초밖에 없으니 기운 바짝차리고 해, 알았어?

pull[get] one's shit together 기운차리다, 정신차리다 = get one's act together

487

You have every right to hate me.

날 증오한대도 난 할 말이 없어.

488

You have gone too far.

네가 너무했어, 심했다.

489

You have good taste in music.

넌 음악에 안목이 있어.

have a good taste in~ …에 조예가 깊다, …에 안목이 있다

490

You have got to be kidding. I do not believe this. 말도 안되는 소리. 난 안믿어.

You've gotta be kidding me 웃기지마, 농담마

491

You have got to get back in the game.
다시 뛰어야지, 다시 한번 싸워야지.

get back in the game 다시 뛰다

492

You have my word.
내 약속하지.

give sb one's word …에게 약속하다 have one's word …의 말을 믿다

493

You have no idea.
넌 모를거야.

494

You have some very large shoes to fill.
너는 매우 막중한 어떤 일을 책임지고 있어.

have large shoes to fill 막중한 책임을 지다

495

You have to get him off the hook.
넌 걔를 곤경에서 구해줘야 해.

get off the hook 곤경에서 벗어나다 get sb off the hook 곤경에서 구해내다

496

You have to get used to it.
적응해야지.

497
You have to throw a party for May.
네가 메이를 위해서 파티를 열어줘야 해.

throw a party 파티를 열다

498
You hear that? I'm getting better.
들었지? 난 점점 좋아지고 있어.

be getting better 점점 나아지다

499
You heard me, son, turn it down!
내 말 들었지, 아들, 소리줄이라고!

You heard me 내 말 알겠지, 내 말 들었잖아

500
You heard what I said. No sex.
내가 한 말 들었지. 섹스는 없어.

You heard what I said 내 말 들었잖아

501
You just freaked out about our relationship.
넌 우리 관계에 대해 놀랬을 뿐이야.

sb freak(ed) out 놀라다, 기겁하다.

502
You just got kicked out of Cornwall for skipping. 넌 학교 빼먹다 코넬에서 쫓겨났잖아.

get kicked out of~ …에서 쫓겨나다

T-Y

503
You just graduated? How about that!
이제 졸업했네? 잘했다!

How about that! 그거 좋은데!, 정말 근사한데!

504
You just have to take my word for it.
너 그거 내 말을 믿어야 돼.

Take my word for it 내 말 진짜야

505
You kissed Chris? I don't believe it!
크리스에게 키스했다고? 말도 안돼!

I don't believe it 말도 안돼, 뜻밖이네

506
You knocked her up, but you're not going to marry her.
걔 임신시켜놓고 결혼은 안 할거라고.

get sb pregnant 임신시키다 = knock sb up, get knocked up 임신하다

507
You know better than that.
알만한 사람이 왜 그런 짓을 해.

508
You know the percentage of bands that make it to the big time?
뮤직밴드가 크게 성공할 확률아니?

make it big 크게 성공하다 = make it to the big time

509

You know what I was thinking? We need more friends. 내가 뭘 생각하고 있었는지 알아? 우린 친구가 더 필요해.

You know what I was thinking? 내가 뭘 생각하고 있었는지 알아?

510

You know what they say? They say you're a fool. 사람들이 뭐라고 하는지 알아? 너보고 바보래.

You know what they say? 사람들이 뭐라고 하는지 알아?

511

You know what? I don't need an apology!

그거 알아? 나 사과는 필요없어!

You know what? 그거 알아?, 저 말이야

512

You know where I am, if you need me.

내가 필요하면 나 어디있는지 알지.

You know where I am 내가 어디 있는지 알지

513

You know, kids get teased, and they get over it. 저 말야, 얘들은 놀림 당하기도 하고 또 그걸 극복하기도 해.

be[get] over it …을 잊다, 극복하다 get over oneself 주제파악하다

514

You let me down. I thought I could trust you.

실망했어. 널 믿을 수 있다고 생각했는데.

let sb down …을 실망시키다

515

You look confused. Shall I walk you through it? 혼란스럽죠? 자세히 설명해줄까요?

walk sb through …에게 자세히 설명하다 = talk sb through

516

You look so good! We're so happy for you.

너 정말 좋아 보여! 네가 잘돼서 기뻐.

I'm so[very] happy for you 네가 잘 돼서 기뻐

517

You look unhappy Vicky. How was your day?

비키, 안 좋아 보여. 오늘 어땠어?

How was your day? 오늘 어땠어?

518

You lost me. I'm not sure what you mean.

못 알아들었어. 무슨 말인지 모르겠어.

You lost me (at~) (…부터) 못 알아들었어

519

You made a mess of things.

네가 이 일을 망쳐놓았어.

make a mess of~ 일을 망치다, 실수하다

520

You make me sick.

너 정말 역겨워.

521
You may not like it, but I did what I had to do.
네가 싫어할지도 모르겠지만, 난 내가 할 일을 했어.

I did what I had to do 내가 해야 할 일을 했어요

522
You might want to do that.
그걸 하는게 좋을거야.

523
You might want to take this seriously.
이걸 신중히 다루어보는게 좋겠어.

take sb[sth] seriously 진지하게 받아들이다

524
You mind if I ask you a few questions?
질문 몇 개 좀 해도 돼?

You mind ~ing? …해도 괜찮겠어? You mind if S+V? …해도 괜찮겠어?

525
You need something to do? Like what?
뭐 해야 할게 있다고? 예를 들면?

Like what? 이를테면 어떻게?, 어떤 거?

526
You need to broach the subject of marriage.
넌 결혼얘기를 꺼내야 돼.

broach the subject 그 주제를 꺼내다, 화제로 …을 꺼내다

527
You need to get off the phone soon.
넌 곧 전화를 끊어야 돼.

get off the phone 전화를 끊다 = switch off one's phone

528
You need to go for it. Go for it! Man up!
넌 한번 시도해봐야 돼. 한번 해봐! 남자답게 해봐!

Go for it! 한번 해봐!, 한번 시도해봐!

529
You never know when he's going to come back. 걔가 언제 돌아올지 모르는 일이야.

You never know 그야 모르지 You never know wh~ …는 모르는 일이야

530
You never learn.
넌 구제불능이야.

531
You put this on, you're good to go.
이거 입어, 나가도 돼.

put on 옷을 입다

532
You ruined my weekend by being drunk all the time. 넌 줄곧 술수정부리며 내 주말을 망쳤어.

ruin one's weekend 주말을 망치다 ruin one's night 저녁시간을 망치다

533
You said it.
네 말이 맞아, 내 말이 그말이야.

534
You saved my ass.
네가 날 살렸어.

save one's ass …을 구해주다

535
You saw a UFO hovering over your house last night? Yeah, I'll bet.
어젯밤에 너희 집 위에서 UFO가 맴도는 걸 봤다구? 그래, 어련하시겠어.

536
You screw up every relationship you've ever been in. 넌 예전 모든 연인관계를 망쳤어.

screw it up 망치다 screw up sth …을 망치다

537
You screwed me!
날 속였군!

538
You see, this would be one of the stupid fights.
있잖아, 이건 한심한 싸움질 중의 하나가 될거야.

you see, 거봐, 있잖아.

539
You should be out and about.
다시 활동을 시작해야지.

be out and about (아픈 후에) 다시 활동을 시작하다

540
You should give yourself credit.
네 공이라는 걸 인정하라구.

541
You should have said no.
넌 거절했어야 했는데.

should have+pp …했어야 했는데 하지 못했다

542
You should know up front this is not a love story. 이건 러브 스토리가 아니라는 것을 미리 아셔야 합니다.

know up front 미리 알다

543
You shouldn't be so hard on her.
넌 걔한테 넘 심하게 하면 안돼.

be hard on sb …을 힘들게 대하다

544
You shouldn't have gone to that trouble.
그렇게까지 애를 쓰지 않아도 됐을텐데.

go to the trouble 애쓰다

545
You still stuck on him, honey?
넌 아직도 걔한테 빠져있니, 애야?

be stuck on sb …에게 빠져있다

546
You still went out and screwed around behind my back. 너 아직도 나가서 내 뒤에서 딴 짓하는거야.

screw around 빈둥거리다, 섹스하고 다니다

547
You succeeded? That's my boy!
네가 성공했다고? 잘했다!

That's my[the] boy! 잘했어!, 좋았어! That's my[the] girl! 잘했어!

548
You suck at this!
너 되게 못하네!

suck at sth[~ing] …에 서투르다, 젬병이다

549
You tell me.
그거야 네가 알지, 네가 더 잘 알지.

550
You tell the truth, you're off the hook.
사실을 말하면 넌 아무 일 없을거야.

be off the hook 무사하다, 면제되다

551
You the man! Great job!
잘했다! 아주 잘했어!
You('re) the man! 잘했다!, 너무 멋져!

552
You think I enjoyed that? Guilty as charged.
내가 그걸 즐겼다고 생각해? 맞아 그랬어.
Guilty (as charged) 어 맞아, 내가 그랬어

553
You think I'm gonna break his heart and mess up your friendship? 내가 걔 맘에 상처주고 네 우정을 망칠거라 생각해?
sb mess it up 망치다, 잘못하다 mess everything up 모든 걸 망치다

554
You think this has nothing to do with you.
넌 이게 너와 아무 관련이 없다고 생각하지.
have a lot to do with~ …와 관련이 많다 ⇔ have nothing to do with~…와 관련이 없다

555
You think you're so smart, don't you?
너 네가 아주 똑똑한 줄 알고 있지, 그렇지 않아?
You think you're~ …한 줄 아는데 그렇지 않아

556
You told me to get a life, remember?
나보고 제대로 살라고 말했잖아, 기억나?
Get a life! 정신차려!, 똑바로 살아!

557

You told me you were going to take me for lunch. 나 점심 사준다고 했잖아.

take sb for~ …을 데리고 …하러가다, …을 …로 (잘못) 생각하다

558

You too. Let's get together again soon.
나도 그래. 곧 다시 만나자.

You too는 나도 그래.(It was nice talking to you too의 준 표현).

559

You took the words right out of my mouth.
내 말이 그 말이야.

560

You turn me on.
넌 내 맘에 쏙 들어, 넌 날 흥분시켜.

turn sb on …을 흥분시키다, …의 몸을 달아오르게 하다 (↔ turn sb off)

561

You two should get a room!
너희 둘 방잡아라!

Get a room! 방잡아라!

562

You up for it?
하고 싶어?, 같이 할래?

563

You used to work for Frankie Flynn?
넌 프랭키 플린 밑에서 일했었지?

「work for+사람[회사]」는 「…를 위해 일을 하다」, 즉 「…에서 일하다」는 뜻. "어디서 일하냐"고 물으려면 Who do you work for?

564

You wanna play hardball?
세게 나오시겠다?

play hardball 원하는 걸 얻기 위해 단호하게 입장을 취하다

565

You wanna run it by me?
나한테 물어볼거야?

run it by sb …에게 물어보다, 상의하다

566

You want a hundred dollars? It's a deal.
100 달러를 원한다고? 그렇게 하자.

It's a deal 그렇게 하자, 좋아 **Deal!** 알았어, 그렇게 하자, 약속한거야

567

You want a piece of me? Is that what you're saying?
나랑 해보겠다는거야? 그 말이야?

Is that what you're saying? 네가 말하는게 그거야?

568
You want a say in this?
이 문제로 말하고 싶어?

want a say in~ 발언권을 원하다

569
You want it done? I'm on it.
그걸 끝내길 바란다고? 내가 할게.

I'm on it 내가 할게

570
You want me to fix you up with Chris?
내가 널 크리스에게 소개시켜줄까?

fix sb up with~ …을 …에게 소개시켜주다

571
You want me to go over there.
나보고 거기 가보라는거지.

572
You want to do this to make up for the past?
과거를 보상하기 위해 이걸 하고 싶은거야?

make up for sth …을 보상하다

573
You want to give it a try?
한번 해보고 싶어?

give it a try 한번 해보다 = give it a go, have a go, give it a shot

574
You want to go there?
그 얘기 듣고 싶어?

Don't go there 그 얘기는 하지 말자

575
You want to leave? That makes one of us.
가고 싶다고? 너나 그렇지.

That makes one of us 너나 그렇지

576
You want to stay here? Be my guest.
여기 남겠다고? 그럼 그렇게 해.

Be my guest 그렇게 해, 그럼

577
You want to talk? You go ahead and talk.
말하고 싶어? 어서 말해봐.

Go ahead 어서 해, 어서 들어 go ahead and+V 어서 …하다

578
You were going for a feelski!
너 가슴만지려고 했지!

579
You were mistaken.
네가 틀렸어.

580
You were so great. You made it!
너 대단했어. 네가 해냈어!

make it 성공하다, 해내다 I made it! 내가 해냈어! = I did it!

581
You were? I didn't see you.
그랬어? 난 널 못봤는데.

You were? 그랬어? You are? 그래?

582
You will get in trouble if you do that.
그렇게 하면 곤란해질거야.

be[get] in trouble 곤경에 처하다 = get oneself in trouble

583
You win.
내가 졌어.

584
You won the first prize. How do you do that?
네가 일등했어. 어떻게 해낸거야?

How do you do that? 어떻게 한거야?

585
You won't bail on me again?
넌 다시는 날 바람맞히지 않을거지?

bail on sb 바람맞히다

586

You won't believe this.
이거 믿지 못할 걸.

587

You wouldn't dare harm me!
어떻게 감히 날 해쳐!

You wouldn't dare! 감히 그렇게는 못하겠지! You wouldn't dare+V 감히 …하지는 못하겠지

588

You wouldn't do that! You aren't tough enough.
그렇게 못할거면서! 그렇게 강인하지도 않잖아.

You wouldn't do that! 그렇게 못할거면서!, 절대 못할 걸!

589

You wouldn't know it to look at her.
걔 겉모습만 봐서는 알 수가 없을거야.

You wouldn't know it to look at~ …의 겉모습만 봐서는 모를거야

590

You('ve) brought this on yourself.
이건 네가 자초한거야.

591

You('ve) got it all wrong.
잘못 알고 있는거야, 잘못 이해하고 있어.

592
You'd better get used to it.
거기에 익숙해져야 해.

You'd better+V …해라 I'd[We'd] better+V …해야 돼

593
You'd do the same for me. Right?
너라도 그렇게 했을거야, 그렇지?

do the same for sb …을 위해 똑같이 하다

594
You'd have done the same thing.
너도 똑같이 했었을거야.

do the same thing 같은 일을 하다, 똑같이 하다

595
You'd have no problem with my talking to him?
내가 걔하고 이야기해도 괜찮겠지?

Do you have problem with sth[sb]? …에 뭐 불만 있어?

596
You'll be sorry later.
나중에 후회할거야.

597
You'll get the hang of it.
금방 손에 익을거야, 요령이 금방 붙을거예요.

598

You'll get the knack of it.
넌 요령이 붙을거야.

have a knack for[of]~ …하는 재주가 있다 = get the hang of~

599

You'll have to leave early if you want to beat the traffic on Friday. **금요일에 교통혼잡을 피하려면 일찍 출발해야 돼.**

beat the traffic 교통혼잡을 피하다

600

You'll make it happen.
성공할거야.

make it happen 그렇게 되도록 하다, 성공하다

601

You'll never get over your broken heart.
넌 실연의 상처를 절대 극복하지 못할거야.

get over sth[sb] 극복하다, 이겨내다, 잊다

602

You're a man about town.
넌 도시의 한량이야.

603

You're already in trouble. There's nothing I can do about it. **넌 이미 곤경에 처했어. 나도 어쩔 도리가 없어.**

(There's) Nothing I can do about it 나도 어쩔 도리가 없어

604
You're better off without me.
나 없는게 너한테 더 좋을거야.

605
You're breaking my heart.
거 참 안됐군요(비아냥거림), 너 때문에 내 가슴이 찢어져.

606
You're catching on.
빨리 이해하는구나.

607
You're cutting it close. You may miss the bus.
너 아슬아슬했어. 버스 놓칠 뻔했어.

cut it close 아슬아슬하다

608
You're doing OK?
잘 지내?, 별 일 없지?

609
You're done here. I need you to leave the room. 넌 끝장이야. 이 방에서 나가줘.

We're done (with) 우리는 (…을) 끝냈어 You're done 넌 끝났어

610
You're driving me crazy.
너 때문에 미치겠어.

611
You're full of it! You never dated my sister!
말도 안돼! 넌 내 누나랑 데이트한 적 없어!

You're so full of it[crap, shit]! 뻥까지마!, 말도 안돼!

612
You're getting warmer. Just a little to the left.
점점 가까워지고 있어. 조금만 더 왼쪽으로.

613
You're going to be all right. Just hang in there.
너 괜찮을거야. 그냥 참고 견뎌.

Hang in there! 참고 견뎌!

614
You're going to do a physical?
건강검진 받을거야?

get[do] a physical 건강검진을 받다   get physical 섹스하다, 폭력을 쓰다

615
You're gonna have to deal with that.
넌 그걸 처리해야 할거야.

deal with 다루다, 처리하다, 견디다, 이겨내다   I can't deal with~ 다루다

616
You're gonna propose to her tonight, aren't you? 너 오늘밤에 걔한테 청혼할거지, 그렇지?

617
You're good to go. Let's leave.
넌 이제 해도 돼. 나가자.

You're good to go 준비가 다 되었으니 해도 된다

618
You're history! It's over!
넌 끝이야! 끝났어!

Sb be history 끝이야, 잊혀진 사람이야

619
You're into material shit.
당신은 하찮은 속물이에요.

620
You're just gonna have to get over it.
이 일을 극복해야 할거야.

get over (어려움 등을) 이겨내다, 슬픔 등을 잊다

621
You're just having a fling with a student?
학생하고 불장난하고 있다는거야?

have a fling with sb 즐섹을 하다 one-night stand[thing] 하룻밤 섹스

622

You're just saying that.
그냥 해보는 소리지, 괜한 소리지.

623

You're kidding me! You expect her to dump me? 설마! 걔가 날 찰거라 생각해?

You're kidding (me) 장난[농담]하는거지 You're not kidding? 정말이구나?

624

You're leaving? I thought you were going to stay. 간다고? 머물거라 생각했는데.

You're leaving? 가?, 그만둬? Are you leaving so soon? 벌써 가는거야?

625

You're looking for someone to sweep you off your feet. 넌 네 마음을 사로잡을 누군가를 찾고 있는거야.

sweep sb off their feet …의 마음을 사로잡다

626

You're lying to me.
거짓말하지마.

627

You're making a fool of yourself.
멍청한 짓을 하는거야.

make a fool of oneself 멍청한 짓을 하다, 웃음거리가 되다

628
You're never gonna fit through there!
저기 좁아서 지나가지 못할거예요!

fit sb (옷 등이) 맞다 fit through 지나가기에 적합하다

629
You're not alone.
너만 그런게 아니야, 넌 혼자가 아니야.

630
You're not going steady with the guy.
넌 걔랑 고정적으로 사귀지 못할거야.

go steady 오랫동안 사귀다

631
You're not so cocky now, are you?
넌 이제 그렇게 거만하게 굴지 않지, 그지?

632
You're not supposed to do that.
그러면 안돼.

633
You're not supposed to stay friends with him.
넌 그와 친구사이가 되면 안돼.

make[stay] friends with~ …와 친구로 사귀다[남다]

634
You're not that way.
넌 그런 사람 아니잖아.

635
You're not the only one that gets a say in this!
너는 이 문제에 말할 권리가 없는 유일한 사람이야!

get[have] a say in~ …에서 말할 권리가 있다

636
You're off the case.
이 환자에서 손떼!, 이 사건에서 손떼.

be off the case 이 사건(환자)에서 손떼다

637
You're offering me fifty dollars? You must be joking.
내게 50달러를 주겠다고? 농담이겠지.

You must be joking 농담이겠지

638
You're on. I can beat you.
좋아. 난 널 이길 수 있어.

You're on (내기) 좋아, 그래. 상대방의 내기 제안 혹은 도전을 받아들이면서 "그래 해보자"라는 의미 참고로 I'm on은 상대방 제의에 찬성할 때 쓰는 표현이다.

639
You're one to talk.
사돈 남 말 하네, 웃기고 있네.

640

You're putting words in my mouth.
넌 내가 하지도 않은 말을 했다는거야.

put words in sb's mouth …가 하지도 않은 말을 했다고 하다

641

You're really starting to creep me out.
넌 정말 날 겁나게 하고 있어.

creep sb out 겁나게 하다 gross sb out 징그럽게 하다

642

You're right on!
좋아!, 맞아!

643

You're scaring me a little bit.
네가 점점 무서워진다.

You're scaring me 네가 무서워진다, 무서워지네

644

You're so fucked up.
너 완전히 좆됐다.

be fucked up하면 「다 엉망이 되다」, 「망치다」라는 뜻. fuck-up은 명사형으로 「실패」, 「얼간이」라는 의미이다.

645

You're so full of crap.
넌 완전 엉터리야.

646

You're so hell bent on winning the contest.
넌 대회에서 우승하기 위해 필사적이야.

be hell bent on sth[~ing] …하는데 필사적이다, …하려고 작정하다

647

You're so messed up.
넌 완전히 엉망이 됐다.

sth[sb] be messed up 엉망이 되다

648

You're still on that?
아직도 그 얘기야?

649

You're still willing to put them through this?
너 아직도 걔네들이 이걸 겪게 할 생각이야?

put ~ through sth …가 …을 겪게 하다

650

You're such a wimp. Listen, if you don't ask her out, I will.
이런 소심한 녀석. 잘들어, 네가 안하면 내가 데이트 신청한다.

651

You're supposed to be in love with me.
넌 나를 사랑하게 되어 있어.

You are(not) supposed to+V …해야 한다, …하면 안된다

652
You're supposed to never talk to the prick again. 넌 절대로 다시는 그 놈하고 얘기하지마라.

653
You're sure you want to go through with this?
너 정말 이러고 싶은거야?

go through with sth 끝까지 완수하다, 관철하다

654
You're telling me he's not just another dumb jock. 걔가 돌대가리가 아니라고 말하는거야?

655
You're telling me you were not a lady's man.
넌 여자 킬러가 아니었다는거야?

656
You're telling me. There's no need to be embarrassed. 정말 그래. 당황해할 필요없어.

You're telling me 정말 그래, 누가 아니래 You're telling me S+V …라는거야?

657
You're up to no good.
쓸데없는 짓을 하고 있구만, 또 이상한 짓을 꾸미고 있구나.

up to no good 쓸모 없는

658
You're welcome to take a look at it.
맘껏 둘러보세요.

You're welcome to+V …해도 돼, …하고 싶으면 해

659
You're welcome. Glad I could help you.
괜찮아. 널 도와줘서 내가 기뻐.

You're welcome 천만에요, 뭘요

660
You've been on my ass all day.
종일 귀찮게 하네.

be on one's ass …을 귀찮게 하다

661
You've been sneaking out in the middle of the night? 넌 한밤 중에 몰래 나간거야?

sneak into~ …로 들어가다

662
You've come a long way.
장족의 발전을 했군.

663
You've gone off the deep end.
넌 정신나갔어, 자제력을 잃었어.

go off the deep end 자제력을 잃다, 이유없이 화를 버럭 내다

664

You've gone too far.
네가 너무했어, 심했어.

665

You've got a point. Let's do that right now.
네 말이 맞아. 당장 그렇게 하자.

You've got a point (there) 네 말이 일리가 있다

666

You've got sex on the brain, you know that?
넌 머릿속에 온통 섹스만 들어있지, 그거 알아?

you know that(?) 너 그거 알잖아, 그거 알아?

667

You've got to go easy on butter and cheese.
버터하고 치즈를 적당히 먹어야 돼.

go easy on[with] sth …을 적당히 하다

668

You've got to play hard to get anywhere in life.
살면서 성과를 얻으려면 열심히 살아야 돼.

play hard to get 튕기다, 비싸게 굴다, 밀당하다

669

You've got to promise that you'll never, ever tell Ken that I told you.
너 절대로 켄한테 내가 말해줬다고 하면 안돼.

never, ever+V 절대로 (그러면 안된다고 거듭 강조하는 표현)

670
You've made your point.
너의 주장이 뭔지 알겠어, 무슨 말인지 알겠어.

671
You've never warmed to me.
넌 나를 따뜻하게 대해준 적이 없었어.

warm (up) to sb[sth] 좋아하기 시작하다

672
Your answers better match up on every account.
여러분의 답변들은 모든 점에서 일치해야 할 겁니다.

Sth better+V …해야 된다

673
Your boss seems unkind, just like mine. Welcome to my world.
네 사장도 우리 사장처럼 퉁명스럽게 보여. 나와 같은 처지가 됐구만.

Welcome to my world 이제 같은 처지군

674
Your ex-wife came by this morning to check up on you.
네 전처가 오늘 아침에 와서 네 상태를 확인했어.

check up on 확인해보다, 지켜보다

675
Your guess is as good as mine.
모르긴 나도 매한가지야.

676

Your life doesn't suck, you have a woman who really loves you. 네 인생은 나쁘지 않아, 널 진정으로 사랑하는 여자가 있잖아.

That sucks! 재수없어!, 젠장헐! You suck! 넌 밥맛이야!

677

Your mother can come live with us.
네 엄마 오셔서 같이 살아도 돼.

can live with sb …와 함께 살다

678

Your roommate's a freak.
네 룸메이트 이상한 놈이네.

679

Your wife is so beautiful. You've got it made.
네 아내 정말 예뻐. 잘 나가는구나.

get it made 성공하다, 잘 풀리다

680

Your word is shot to hell now, don't you think?
이제 네 말은 의미가 없어졌어, 그렇지 않아?

be shot to hell 엉망이 되다, 가치가 없어지다

Check it Out!
문장속에서 확인해보기!

A: Oh, excuse me. I seem to have stepped on your foot.
B: That's all right. Don't let it bother you.

A: 어머, 미안해요. 제가 당신 발을 밟은 듯 하군요.
B: 괜찮아요. 신경쓰지 마세요.

Don't let it bother you
Don't let+목적어+동사로 쓰이면 목적어가 동사를 하지 못하도록 하다라는 뜻이 된다.

A: Did you see that guy? What an idiot!
B: Hey, **take it easy.** No need to become so angry while you're driving.

A: 저놈 봤어? 이런 멍청이 같으니라구!
B: 야, 진정해. 운전중에 그렇게 화낼 필요 뭐 있어.

What an idiot?
감탄문을 만들 때는 How+형용사!, 혹은 여기서처럼 What a+명사!로 간단히 쓰면 된다.

A: My girlfriend broke up with me this weekend.
B: That's too bad. Let me buy you a drink after work.

A: 이번 주말에 여자친구랑 깨졌어.
B: 안됐다. 내가 퇴근 후 한잔 살게.

break up with
헤어지다라는 의미. break는 뭔가 지속되다가 멈추다는 뜻을 갖는 단어로 coffee break에서 break는 휴식을 의미한다.

A: You look so depressed. **What's wrong with you?**
B: Samantha said she wanted to break up with me. What should I do?

look so depressed
look은 뒤에 형용사가 오면서 2형식 동사로 자주 쓰인다. '…처럼 보이다'라는 의미이다. 의미는 '울쩍해보이다'라는 뜻이다.

A: 너 기분이 안좋아 보인다. 무슨 일 있어?
B: 사만다가 나하고 헤어지고 싶대. 어떻게 해야 하지?

A: How could you do this to me?
B: **That's enough!** I said I'm sorry more than a thousand times!!

I said that~
뭔가 자기가 전에 말했다고 강조할 때 쓰는 표현으로 I told you that~이라고도 한다. 물론 두 경우 모두 that은 생략될 수 있다.

A: 어떻게 나한테 이럴 수가 있어?
B: 그만 좀 해! 수천번도 더 미안하다고 했잖아!!

A: What should I wear to the party tonight?
B: It's up to you. I can't decide for you.
A: **Why not?**

It's up to you.
너에게 달린 문제라는 뜻으로 어떤 문제인지 구체적으로 함께 말하려면 It's up to you to+V의 형태로 써주면 된다. 예로 "결정하는 건 너에게 달렸어"라고 하려면 It's up to you to decide라고 하면 된다.

A: 오늘 밤 파티에 뭘 입고 가는게 좋을까?
B: 그거야 네 맘이지. 내가 대신 정해줄 순 없다구.
A: 안될 건 또 뭐 있어?

memo

후다닥 스크린영어
대표문장 2500

SUPPLEMENT

영화 속 명대사

노트북에서 노아

I could be whatever you want. You just tell me what you want and I'll be that for you.

난 네가 원하는 무엇이든 돼 줄 수 있어. 네가 원하는 게 뭔지만 말해. 내가 널 위해 그렇게 되어 줄게.

미비포유에서 루이스

You only get one life. It's actually your duty to live it as fully as possible.

인생은 한번뿐이에요. 최대한 충실히 사는 게 삶에 대한 당신의 의무예요.

이보다 더 좋을 수는 없다에서 멜빈

You make me want to be a better man.

당신 때문에 난 좀더 나은 남자가 되고 싶어졌다구요.

미비포유에서 윌

Do you know something, Clark? You are pretty much the only thing that makes me want to get up in the morning.

클락, 그거 알아요? 아침에 일어나고 싶은 유일한 이유는 당신이 있기 때문이에요.

> 러브 로지에서 알렉스

What I once said about you is still true, there's nothing you can't do if you put your mind to it. So keep chasing those dreams, will you, darling?

내가 전에 너에 대해 말한 것은 여전히 사실이야. 넌 마음만 먹으면 못할 일이 없어. 그러니 그 꿈을 절대 포기하지마, 알았지?

> 비포 선라이즈에서 제시

Whatever happens tomorrow, we've had today.

내일 무슨 일이 일어나든, 우리는 오늘을 함께 였어.

> 이프 온리에서 이안

Thank you for being the person who taught me to love and to be loved.

사랑하는 법을, 그리고 사랑받는 법을 가르쳐줘서 고마워.

> 플래툰에서 테일러

I think now, looking back, we did not fight the enemy. We fought ourselves and the enemy was in us.

되돌아보면, 우리는 적과 싸운 것이 아니었다. 우리는 우리 자신과 싸웠고, 적은 우리 안에 있었다.

> 제리 맥과이어에서 로드

I just want to make sure you're ready, brother. Here it is: "Show me the money!"

마음의 준비는 됐겠지, 친구. 자…, "돈을 보여줘!"

> 더티 해리에서 해리

Go ahead, make my day.

덤벼봐, 오늘 하루 신나게 해줘.

> 오즈의 마법사에서 도로시

There's no place like home.

집만 한 곳은 없지.

> 장미가의 전쟁에서 올리버

I think you owe me an apology, Barbara. If you have something to say, I'd like to hear it.

나에게 사과해야 되지 않나, 바바라? 할 말이 있다면 해 봐.

> 대부에서 마이클

Keep your friends close, but your enemies closer.

친구는 가까이, 그러나 적은 더 가까이.

> 죽은 시인의 사회에서 존

Carpe diem. Seize the day, boys. Make your lives extraordinary.

오늘을 붙잡아라, 얘들아. 너희들의 삶을 특별하게 만들어라.

> 아이언맨에서 토니

If we can't accept limitations, then we're no better than the bad guys.

만약 우리가 한계를 인정하지 못한다면, 우리 또한 나쁜 놈들과 다름없어.

> 포레스트 검프에서 포레스트

Life is like a box of chocolates, you never know what you're going to get.

인생은 초콜릿 상자와도 같아. 무엇을 집게 될 지는 먹기 전에 절대 알 수 없어.

> 에덴의 동쪽에서 칼

It's awful not to be loved, it's the worst thing in the world.

사랑받지 못한다는 것은 이 세상에서 가장 괴로운 것이다.

> 스파이더맨에서 벤 삼촌

Great power always comes with Great responsibility.

강한 힘에는 그만큼의 책임이 따른다.

> 라라랜드에서 미아

People will want to go to it because you're passionate about it, and people love what other people are passionate about. You remind people of what they forgot.

사람들은 당신이 열정적이기 때문에 당신 재즈클럽에 가고 싶어할거예요. 사람들은 다른 사람들의 열정에 끌리게 되어 있어요. 자신들이 잊었던 것을 상기시켜주니까요.

> 500일의 썸머에서 썸머

I just don't feel comfortable being anyone's girlfriend. I don't actually feel comfortable being anyone's anything, you know. … I like being on my own. Relationships are messy, and people's feelings get hurt. Who needs it?

난 누군가의 여친이 되는 게 불편해요. 사실 누군가의 뭔가가 되는 것 자체가 편하지 않아요…. 난 내 자신으로 존재하고 싶어. 사람들 관계라는게 혼란스럽고 사람들의 감정은 상처를 받게 되는데 누가 그걸 원해?

> 노트북에서 노아

Would you stop thinking about what everyone wants. Stop thinking about what I want, what he wants, what your parents want. What do you want? What do you want?

모든 사람이 원하는 것을 만족시켜줄 수는 없어. 내가 원하는 거, 그가 원하는 거, 네 부모님이 원하는 거는 생각하지마. 넌 뭘 원하는데? 뭘 원하는데?

> 로맨틱 홀러데이에서 아서와 아이리스

**Arthur: Iris, in the movies we have leading ladies…
…and we have the best friend. You, I can tell, are a leading lady. But for some reason, you're behaving like the best friend.
Iris: You're so right. You're supposed to be the leading lady of your own life, for God's sake.**

아서: 아이리스, 영화에서는 여주인공들이 있고 그리고 조연도 있어요. 내가 보기에 아가씨는 여주인공인데 어떤 이유에서인지 조연처럼 행동하고 있어요.
아이리스: 선생님이 말이 맞아요. 정말이지 자기 인생에서는 자신이 주인공이 되어야 해요.

> 미비포유에서 윌

You are scored on my heart, Clark. You were, from the first day you walked in. With your sweet smile and your ridiculous clothes. And your bad jokes, and your complete inability to ever hide a single thing that you felt. Don't think of me too often. I do not want you getting sad. Just live well. Just live. I'll be walking beside you every step of the way.

클락, 당신은 내 마음에 새겨져 있어요. 어여쁜 미소를 띄고 우스꽝스러운 옷차림으로 내게 걸어 들어오던 그 첫날부터 그랬어요. 당신의 엉뚱한 농담들, 속마음을 하나도 숨기지 못하는 것까지. 내 생각 너무 자주 하지 말아요. 당신이 슬퍼지는 건 원하지 않아요. 그냥 잘 살아요. 그냥 살아요. 내가 매 순간 당신과 함께 할게요.

> 프렌즈 위드 베네핏에서 딜런의 아버지

I'll tell you something that I wish I knew when I was your age. And I know you've heard a million times, "life is short." But let me tell you something, what this is teaching me is that life is goddamn short and you can't waste a minute of it.

내가 네 나이에 알고 싶었던 걸 말해줄게. 인생이 짧다는건 수없이 들었지? 근데 이 병(치매)의 교훈이 뭔지 말해줄까? 인생은 빌어먹게도 짧아서 단 1분도 낭비할 수 없다는거야.

> 어바웃 타임에서 팀

We're all travelling through time together every day of our lives. All we can do is do our best to relish this remarkable ride.

우리 모두는 매일 함께 시간을 보내며 여행을 하고 있다. 우리가 할 수 있는 건 최선을 다해 이 멋진 여정을 즐기는 것이다.

`미비포유에서 윌`

That is why I can't have you tied to me. I don't want you to miss all the things that someone else could give you. And selfishly I don't want you to look at me one day and feel even the tiniest big of regret or pity.

바로 그래서 당신을 내게 얽매이게 할 수 없어요. 누군가 당신에게 해줄 수 있는 것들을 당신이 놓치는 것을 원치 않아요. 그리고 이기적이게도, 난 어느날 당신이 날 보고 조금이나마 후회나 연민을 느끼는 것을 원치 않아요.

`첫키스만 50번째에서 루시`

Nothing beats a first kiss. There's nothing like a first kiss.

첫키스가 최고예요. 첫키스만큼 좋은 것은 없어요.

`어바웃 타임의 팀`

The truth is, I now don't travel back at all. Not even for the day. I just try to live every day as if I've deliberately come back to this one day to enjoy it as if it was the full final day of my extraordinary, ordinary life.

사실은 난 이제 시간여행을 하지 않는다. 단 하루도 돌아가지 않는다. 나는 단지 매일 살려고 노력한다. 내 특별하고도 평범한 인생의 마지막날 인 듯, 즐기기 위해 일부러 과거로 돌아온 날인 것처럼 말이다.

> 친구와 연인사이에서 엠마와 아담

Emma: I don't know why I wasted so much time pretending I didn't care. I guess I just didn't want to feel like this. It hurts. But I love you. I'm totally and completely in love with you, and I don't care if you think it's too late, I'm telling you anyway… You should know…
Adam: If you come any closer, I'm not letting you go.

엠마: 왜 내가 신경 안쓰는 척하면서 시간을 그렇게 많이 낭비했는지 몰라. 그렇게 느끼는 걸 원하지 않았던 것 같아. 가슴이 아파. 하지만 널 사랑해. 완전히 널 사랑한다고. 그리고 너무 늦었다고 네가 생각해도 난 상관없어. 너한테 말하고 싶었으니까.

아담: 조금만 더 가까이 오면, 다신 널 떠나지 못하게 할거야.

> 노트북에서 노아

I am no one special, just a common man with common thoughts. I've led a common life. There are no monuments dedicated to me. And my name will soon be forgotten. But in one respect, I've succeeded as gloriously as anyone who ever lived. I've loved another with all my heart and soul and for me that has always been enough.

난 특별한 사람이 아니다. 그저 평범한 사람이다. 남다른 인생을 산 것도 아니고. 날 기리는 기념탑도 없을 것이고 내 이름은 곧 잊혀질게다. 하지만 한 가지 면에서는 난 세상 어느 누구보다 눈부신 성공을 했다. 난 내 모든 영혼과 마음을 바쳐 한사람을 사랑했으니, 이걸로 충분히 내 삶은 성공한 인생이야.

`어바웃 타임의 팀의 아버지`

We're all quite similar in the end. We all get old and tell the same tales too many times. But try and marry someone kind.

인생은 결국 다 비슷해진다. 모두 늙어서 지난 날을 추억하는 것일 뿐이다. 하지만 결혼은 따뜻한 사람하고 하거라.

`미비포유에서 윌`

I get that this could be a good life. but it's not, "My life." It's not even close. You never saw me, before. I loved my life. I've really loved it.

이렇게 사는 것도 괜찮을 수 있겠죠. 하지만 그건 내 인생이 아녜요. 전혀 아니에요. 전에 나의 모습을 본 적이 없잖아요. 난 내 인생을 정말 사랑했어요.

`어퓨굿맨 중에서`

Kaffe: I want the truth!

Colonel Jessep: You can't handle the truth! Son, we live in a world that has walls. And those walls have to be guarded by men with guns. Who's going to do it? You? You, Lieutenant Weinberg? I have a greater responsibility than you can possibly fathom. You weep for Santiago and you curse the Marines. You have that luxury. You have that luxury of not knowing what I know. That Santiago's death, while tragic, probably saved lives. And my existence, while grotesque and incomprehensible to you, saves lives. You don't want the truth because deep down in places you don't talk about at parties, you want me on that wall. You need me on that wall. We use words like honor, code, loyalty. We use these words, as the

backbone of a life spent defending something. You use them as a punch line. I have neither the time nor the inclination to explain myself to a man who rises and sleeps under the blanket of the very freedom that I provide and then questions the manner in which I provide it. I would rather you just said "thank you" and went on your way. Otherwise I suggest you pick up a weapon and stand the post. Either way I don't give a damn what you think you are entitled to!

Kaffe: Did you order the Code Red?

Colonel Jessep: I did the job…

Kaffe: Did you order the Code Red?

Colonel Jessep: You're goddamn right I did!

캐피: 난 진실을 듣고 싶어요!
제섭 대령: 자넨 그 진실을 감당할 수 없어. 이봐 애송이, 우린 담장을 빙 두르고 사는 거야. 그 담장을 총을 들고 지켜야 하는 거야. 그런데 그걸 누가 할 건가? 자네가? 웨인버그 중위, 자네가? 내 책임이 얼마나 막중한지 자넨 알래야 알 수 없어. 자넨 산티아고를 불쌍히 여기면서 우리 해병대 험담이나 하겠지. 속 편해, 내가 알고 있는 걸 모르니 자넨 속 편할 거야. 그 사병이 죽은건 물론 비극적인 일이긴 하지만 다른 사람들을 살렸어. 그리고 내가 사령관이라는 게 자네에겐 괴상하고 이해되지 않겠지만 그래서 모두 살아있는 거라구. 자넨 마음 깊숙한 곳에서, 그런 거에 관해서 파티장에서 떠들지도 않겠지만, 날 그 담장에 내가 있어주길 바라는 거야. 자넨 내가 거기 있어야만 해. 그래서 자넨 진실을 알고 싶지 않을 거야. 우리들은 명예, 규칙, 충성 같은 말을 하지. 어떤 것을 지키느라 평생을 보낸 우리같은 사람은 그 말을 절대절명의 의미로 쓰는 거야. 자네같은 사람들은 농담할 때나 쓰지. 난 내가 던져준 바로 그 자유의 이불을 덮고 자고 일어나서는, 어떤 방식으로 제공했는지를 의문을 제기하는 사람에게 대답할 만한 시간도 없고 대답하고 싶은 생각도 없어. "고맙습니다"라고 말하고 그냥 자네 갈 길을 가는 게 좋아. 그렇지 않으면 무기들고 보초를 서든지. 어쨌건, 네가 대답들을 자격이 있다고 생각하는 것 따위엔 난 관심없어!
캐피: 귀관이 「코드레드」를 명령했습니까?
제섭 대령: 임무를 수행했을 뿐이야.
캐피: 귀관이 「코드레드」를 명령했습니까?
제섭 대령: 그래, 내가 했다!

memo